I0504788

Mastering Social Media:

10 Powerful Strategies to Outsmart Algorithms and Skyrocket Your Growth

Subtitle: Unlocking the Secrets of the
Social Media Universe

Summary:

In "Mastering Social Media: 10 Powerful Strategies to Outsmart
Algorithms and Skyrocket Your Growth," we explore the ever-

evolving world of social media and its algorithms to help you better understand and navigate the digital landscape. The book presents ten distinct strategies designed to help you gain a competitive edge on social media platforms, beat the algorithms, and grow your online audience exponentially. By focusing on key aspects such as content creation, engagement, analytics, and platform-specific tips, this book offers a comprehensive guide to mastering social media and achieving your digital goals.

Chapter 1: Unleashing the Power of High-Quality Content

1. Crafting Compelling Stories

2. Embracing Visual Storytelling

3. Consistency: The Key to Content Success

4. Discovering Your Unique Voice

5. Diversifying Your Content Portfolio

Chapter 2: Building Authentic Relationships

1. Engaging with Your Audience

2. Collaborating with Influencers

3. Harnessing User-Generated Content

4. Creating a Community Around Your Brand

5. Responding to Feedback and Criticism

Chapter 3: Mastering the Art of Hashtags

1. Decoding Hashtag Science

2. Choosing the Right Hashtags for Your Content

3. Balancing Broad and Niche Hashtags

4. Tracking Hashtag Performance

5. Creating Branded Hashtags

Chapter 4: Driving Growth with Analytics

1. Analyzing Key Performance Indicators

2. Interpreting Audience Insights

3. Adjusting Your Strategy Based on Data

4. A/B Testing for Maximum Impact

5. Leveraging Social Media Management Tools

Chapter 5: Platform-Specific Tips and Tricks

1. Mastering Instagram's Algorithm

2. Winning the Facebook Game

3. Conquering Twitter's Fast-Paced Landscape

4. Capitalizing on LinkedIn's Professional Network

5. Exploring Emerging Platforms

Chapter 6: Captivating Content through Video

1. Embracing the Power of Video

2. Understanding Video Formats and Platforms

3. Creating Engaging Video Concepts

4. Editing Techniques for Maximum Impact

5. Live Streaming for Real-Time Connection

Chapter 7: The Art of Social Listening

1. Defining Social Listening

2. Monitoring Conversations and Trends

3. Identifying Influencers and Opportunities

4. Adapting to Real-Time Feedback

5. Integrating Social Listening into Your Strategy

Chapter 8: Succeeding with Paid Advertising

1. Exploring the World of Social Media Ads

2. Crafting a Successful Ad Campaign

3. Targeting Your Ideal Audience

4. Optimizing Ad Performance

5. Measuring Return on Investment

Chapter 9: Navigating the Legal Landscape

1. Understanding Copyright and Intellectual Property

2. Complying with Advertising Regulations

3. Protecting Your Brand and Reputation

4. Addressing Privacy and Security Concerns

5. Staying Informed on Legal Changes

Chapter 10: Future-Proofing Your Social Media Strategy

1. Embracing Platform Changes and Updates

2. Adapting to Evolving User Behaviour

3. Experimenting with Emerging Technologies

4. Continuously Learning and Updating Your Skills

5. Cultivating a Growth Mindset and Embracing Innovation

Chapter 1: Unleashing the Power of High-Quality Content

In the ever-changing world of social media, high-quality content remains a constant driving force behind success. This chapter delves into the art of creating compelling, engaging content that not only captures your audience's attention but also encourages them to interact with your brand. Let's begin with the foundation of every great piece of content: crafting a compelling story.

1.1 Crafting Compelling Stories

A captivating story is at the heart of every piece of content that resonates with audiences. A well-crafted narrative can evoke emotions, spark curiosity, and create memorable experiences. Here are some essential tips to help you craft compelling stories for your social media channels:

1. Identify your target audience: Before you begin, it's crucial to have a clear understanding of your target audience. What are their interests, pain points, and desires? By knowing your audience, you can create stories that speak directly to them, ensuring your content resonates and drives engagement.

2. Define your message: What do you want your audience to take away from your story? Establishing a clear message allows you to create focused and purposeful content. Whether you're looking to

inspire, educate, or entertain, make sure your message aligns with your brand's values and goals.

3. Create a strong narrative structure: A well-structured story is easier to follow and more enjoyable for your audience. Begin with a hook that grabs their attention, followed by the main body of your story, and end with a compelling conclusion that leaves a lasting impression. Remember, the goal is to engage your audience from start to finish.

4. Develop relatable characters: Incorporate characters into your story that your audience can relate to and connect with. This can be a real person, a fictional persona, or even your brand as a whole. The more your audience can empathize with the characters in your story, the more emotionally invested they'll become.

5. Evoke emotion: People are more likely to remember and share content that evokes strong emotions. Use descriptive language, visuals, and sounds to create an emotional response from your audience. Whether it's happiness, sadness, or surprise, emotional storytelling can leave a lasting impact.

6. Keep it authentic: Authenticity is key to connecting with your audience on a deeper level. Share real stories, experiences, and insights that align with your brand's identity. Being genuine and honest will foster trust and loyalty among your followers.

By incorporating these storytelling techniques into your content creation process, you can craft compelling stories that not only engage your audience but also drive meaningful conversations around your brand. In the following sections, we'll explore other aspects of high-quality content, including visual storytelling, consistency, finding your unique voice, and diversifying your content portfolio.

1.2 Embracing Visual Storytelling

As the saying goes, "A picture is worth a thousand words." In the world of social media, this couldn't be more accurate. Visual storytelling is a powerful tool that can help you convey your message more effectively and leave a lasting impact on your audience. In this section, we'll explore the importance of visual storytelling and offer tips on how to incorporate it into your content strategy.

1. Understand the power of visuals: Visuals are processed much faster by the human brain than text, making them an essential component of effective storytelling. High-quality visuals can evoke emotions, clarify complex concepts, and strengthen your narrative. By incorporating images, videos, and other visual elements into your content, you can create a more immersive and memorable experience for your audience.

2. Choose the right visuals: Not all visuals are created equal. To maximize the impact of your visual storytelling, choose images and videos that are relevant to your message, high-quality, and visually appealing. Consider using a mix of photographs, illustrations, infographics, and videos to keep your content fresh and engaging.

3. Align visuals with your brand identity: Your visuals should reflect your brand's personality and values. Use a consistent color

palette, typography, and style to create a cohesive look and feel across all your content. This helps reinforce your brand identity and makes your content more recognizable to your audience.

4. Make visuals shareable: Social media platforms are designed for sharing, so create visuals that are easily shareable and encourage your audience to spread your message. This could include creating infographics with interesting facts, designing quote images, or sharing behind-the-scenes photos that give your followers a glimpse into your world.

5. Optimize visuals for each platform: Each social media platform has its unique requirements and best practices when it comes to visuals. For example, vertical images perform better on Pinterest, while square images are more suited to Instagram. Familiarize yourself with the optimal image sizes and formats for each platform, and tailor your visuals accordingly.

6. Don't forget about accessibility: Ensure that your visuals are accessible to all users, including those with visual impairments. Add descriptive alt-text to your images, use high-contrast colors, and avoid relying solely on visuals to convey important information.

By embracing visual storytelling, you can enhance your content's appeal and make your brand more memorable. In the following sections, we'll discuss the importance of consistency in your content, discovering your unique voice, and diversifying your content portfolio to keep your audience engaged and coming back for more.

1.3 Consistency: The Key to Content Success

Consistency is a vital component of a successful social media strategy. Maintaining a steady presence on your chosen platforms not only helps you stay top-of-mind for your audience but also signals to social media algorithms that your content is relevant and valuable. In this section, we'll discuss the importance of consistency in your content strategy and offer tips on how to achieve it.

1. Create a content calendar: Planning your content in advance ensures that you maintain a consistent posting schedule. A content calendar allows you to organize your content ideas, track important dates and events, and allocate resources more effectively. By planning ahead, you can avoid last-minute stress and ensure that you always have fresh content to share with your audience.

2. Set realistic goals: Consistency doesn't mean you have to post every single day. Instead, set achievable goals based on your available resources and current audience engagement. Determine the optimal posting frequency for your brand and strive to maintain it. Over time, you can adjust your goals as your audience grows and your resources expand.

3. Establish a consistent brand voice: Your brand voice is the unique personality and tone that comes across in your content.

Maintaining a consistent voice helps your audience recognize your brand and feel more connected to it. Identify the key traits and characteristics that define your brand's voice, and make sure they're reflected in every piece of content you create.

4. Automate where possible: Utilizing scheduling tools and automation can help you maintain consistency with less effort. Many social media management tools allow you to schedule posts in advance and automatically share them at optimal times. By automating some aspects of your content strategy, you can free up more time to focus on creating high-quality content and engaging with your audience.

5. Monitor and adjust: Regularly review your content performance to identify trends and areas for improvement. Analyze your engagement metrics, such as likes, comments, and shares, to determine which types of content resonate most with your audience. Use this information to fine-tune your strategy and maintain consistency in the quality and relevance of your content.

6. Be prepared for change: While consistency is crucial, it's also essential to be adaptable. Social media platforms and audience preferences are constantly evolving, so be prepared to adjust your strategy as needed. Stay informed about new features, best practices, and emerging trends to ensure your content remains fresh and engaging.

By prioritizing consistency in your content strategy, you can establish a reliable presence on social media, build trust with your audience, and increase the likelihood of algorithmic success. In the following sections, we'll discuss discovering your unique voice and diversifying your content portfolio to create a well-rounded and engaging social media presence.

1.4 Discovering Your Unique Voice

Your unique voice is a key factor that sets your brand apart from competitors and helps you forge deeper connections with your audience. A distinctive and consistent brand voice allows your content to be easily recognized and creates a sense of familiarity for your followers. In this section, we'll discuss the importance of finding your unique voice and provide tips on how to refine it.

1. Define your brand personality: Start by identifying the key characteristics that define your brand's personality. Are you fun and quirky, or serious and professional? Consider your target audience, company values, and mission statement to help guide your brand personality development.

2. Create a brand voice guide: Document your brand voice by creating a comprehensive guide that outlines the tone, style, and language you'll use in your content. This guide should include specific examples and guidelines to ensure that your voice remains consistent across all channels and content types.

3. Experiment with different styles: It's essential to find a voice that feels authentic and resonates with your audience. Don't be afraid to experiment with different styles, tones, and language until you find the perfect fit. Pay close attention to audience engagement and feedback to help you refine your voice.

4. Showcase your expertise: Your unique voice should reflect your knowledge and expertise in your industry or niche. By sharing valuable insights, tips, and advice, you can establish yourself as a thought leader and further differentiate your brand from competitors.

5. Be authentic and transparent: An authentic voice is more relatable and trustworthy, which can lead to stronger connections with your audience. Share your brand's story, values, and mission with openness and honesty. This will not only help you find your unique voice but also foster loyalty and trust among your followers.

6. Adapt your voice for different platforms: While maintaining consistency is crucial, it's also essential to adapt your voice to suit the specific platform you're using. For example, a more informal and conversational tone might work well on Twitter, while a professional and polished voice may be more appropriate on LinkedIn. Understand the nuances of each platform and adjust your voice accordingly.

By discovering and refining your unique voice, you can create a more compelling and engaging social media presence that resonates with your audience. In the next section, we'll discuss the importance of diversifying your content portfolio to keep your followers engaged and attract new audiences.

1.5 Diversifying Your Content Portfolio

A diverse content portfolio is essential for maintaining audience engagement and attracting new followers. By offering a mix of content formats and types, you can appeal to a wider range of interests, preferences, and learning styles, ensuring your content remains fresh and engaging. In this section, we'll discuss the importance of content diversification and provide tips on how to achieve it.

1. Experiment with various formats: Social media platforms support a wide range of content formats, including images, videos, articles, and polls. Experiment with different formats to discover which ones resonate most with your audience and align best with your brand's goals. This could include short-form videos, long-form articles, or eye-catching infographics.

2. Share user-generated content: User-generated content (UGC) is a powerful way to diversify your content portfolio while also building trust and fostering a sense of community among your followers. Encourage your audience to create and share content related to your brand, and feature their contributions on your social media channels.

3. Leverage storytelling techniques: Incorporate storytelling elements into your content to create a more engaging and immersive experience for your audience. This could include

sharing case studies, success stories, or behind-the-scenes insights that showcase your brand's personality and values.

4. Educate, entertain, and inspire: Aim to strike a balance between educational, entertaining, and inspirational content. By offering a mix of informative articles, fun visuals, and thought-provoking quotes, you can appeal to a wider range of interests and keep your audience engaged.

5. Collaborate with others: Collaborations with influencers, industry experts, and other brands can help you diversify your content and reach new audiences. Consider partnering on a project, hosting a joint webinar, or conducting an interview to create fresh, engaging content that appeals to both your existing followers and potential new fans.

6. Monitor and adjust: Regularly review your content performance to identify trends, areas for improvement, and opportunities for diversification. Use analytics to determine which types of content perform best and make data-driven decisions about what to include in your content mix moving forward.

By diversifying your content portfolio, you can keep your audience engaged, attract new followers, and ensure that your social media presence remains fresh and dynamic. As you progress through the remaining chapters of this book, you'll continue to explore strategies for beating the algorithm, mastering each social media platform, and ultimately achieving exponential growth for your brand.

Chapter 2: Building Authentic Relationships

One of the most crucial aspects of social media success is fostering genuine connections with your audience. Building authentic relationships not only helps to create a loyal community of followers but also encourages engagement, word-of-mouth referrals, and long-term growth. In this chapter, we'll explore strategies for building and nurturing authentic relationships with your audience, starting with engaging with them on a personal level.

2.1 Engaging with Your Audience

Interacting with your audience is key to forming authentic connections and demonstrating that you value their opinions and insights. Here are some effective strategies to engage with your audience and build lasting relationships:

1. Respond to comments and messages: Make an effort to respond to comments and direct messages from your followers in a timely manner. This shows your audience that you're listening and genuinely care about their thoughts and feedback. Personalized responses can help create a deeper connection and foster loyalty among your followers.

2. Ask for feedback: Encourage your audience to share their

opinions and suggestions by actively seeking their feedback. This can be done through polls, surveys, or simply asking open-ended questions in your captions or stories. Listening to your audience's feedback not only helps you improve your content but also demonstrates that you value their input.

3. Host Q&A sessions: Regularly hosting live Q&A sessions or "Ask Me Anything" events can help you connect with your audience on a more personal level. This allows your followers to ask questions, share their thoughts, and get to know you or your brand better, fostering a sense of community and trust.

4. Share user-generated content: As mentioned earlier, sharing user-generated content (UGC) not only diversifies your content portfolio but also helps build authentic relationships with your audience. By featuring your followers' content, you show your appreciation for their contributions and encourage others to engage with your brand.

5. Organize contests and giveaways: Hosting contests and giveaways can be an effective way to increase engagement and build excitement around your brand. Be sure to clearly outline the rules, provide an enticing prize, and encourage your audience to participate by sharing, commenting, or tagging friends.

6. Celebrate milestones together: Share your achievements and milestones with your audience, and thank them for their support

along the way. This creates a sense of shared accomplishment and reinforces the idea that your followers are an integral part of your brand's success.

By actively engaging with your audience and fostering a two-way dialogue, you can build authentic relationships that contribute to long-term growth and success on social media. In the following sections, we'll discuss the importance of understanding your audience's needs, personalizing your content, and nurturing brand advocates to further strengthen your relationships with your followers.

2.2 Collaborating with Influencers

Influencer collaborations can be a highly effective way to expand your reach, tap into new audiences, and build authentic relationships with both influencers and their followers. When done right, influencer partnerships can generate buzz, drive engagement, and even boost sales. In this section, we'll discuss strategies for successful influencer collaborations and how they can contribute to building authentic relationships.

1. Identify the right influencers: Start by finding influencers who align with your brand values, have a strong connection with their audience, and boast an engaged following in your target demographic. Research their content and engagement metrics to ensure they're a good fit for your brand and objectives.

2. Build genuine connections: Before approaching an influencer for a collaboration, take the time to engage with their content and establish a rapport. This helps create a foundation of trust and mutual respect, which can lead to a more successful and authentic partnership.

3. Set clear goals and expectations: Clearly outline your goals for the collaboration and ensure that both parties understand their roles and responsibilities. Establish a timeline, deliverables, and any relevant guidelines to ensure a smooth and successful partnership.

4. Co-create content: Collaborate with the influencer to create content that resonates with both your audience and theirs. This can include social media posts, blog articles, videos, or even a joint product or service offering. By co-creating content, you can showcase your brand's personality and values, while also benefiting from the influencer's unique perspective and expertise.

5. Offer value to the influencer: Ensure that the collaboration benefits both parties by offering value to the influencer, such as exposure to your audience, access to exclusive resources, or financial compensation. This helps foster a mutually beneficial partnership and lays the groundwork for potential future collaborations.

6. Measure and analyze results: Track the performance of your influencer collaboration by monitoring engagement metrics, referral traffic, and any other relevant key performance indicators (KPIs). Use this data to evaluate the success of the partnership and identify areas for improvement in future collaborations.

By collaborating with influencers in a strategic and authentic way, you can build valuable relationships, expand your reach, and strengthen your brand's presence on social media. In the next section, we'll discuss the importance of understanding your audience's needs and personalizing your content to foster even deeper connections with your followers.

2.3 Harnessing User-Generated Content

User-generated content (UGC) is a powerful tool for building authentic relationships with your audience, fostering a sense of community, and diversifying your content portfolio. By encouraging and showcasing your followers' contributions, you can create a more engaging social media presence and cultivate brand loyalty. In this section, we'll discuss strategies for harnessing user-generated content and leveraging it to strengthen your relationships with your audience.

1. Encourage content creation: Invite your followers to create content related to your brand, product, or service. This can be done through campaigns, contests, or simply by asking them to share their experiences using a specific hashtag. Make sure to communicate the benefits of participating, such as the chance to be featured on your social media channels or win a prize.

2. Set clear guidelines: Provide your audience with clear guidelines and expectations for user-generated content. This can include themes, hashtags, or content formats. Offering guidance helps ensure that the content aligns with your brand values and maintains a consistent look and feel.

3. Acknowledge and share UGC: Regularly acknowledge and share user-generated content on your social media channels. This not only provides fresh and engaging content for your followers but

also shows your appreciation for their contributions. Be sure to give proper credit by tagging the original creator in your posts.

4. Showcase UGC in various formats: User-generated content can be incorporated into your content mix in various formats, such as blog posts, videos, or even promotional materials. For example, you could create a video montage of your followers using your product or write a blog post featuring their testimonials and success stories.

5. Engage with creators: Interact with the creators of user-generated content by liking, commenting, and sharing their posts. This helps to strengthen your relationship with them and encourages others to create and share their own content related to your brand.

6. Monitor and moderate: Keep an eye on the user-generated content related to your brand to ensure it aligns with your values and guidelines. While most UGC will be positive, be prepared to address any negative content or feedback in a professional and constructive manner.

By harnessing user-generated content and incorporating it into your social media strategy, you can create a more engaging and authentic online presence, while building stronger relationships with your audience. In the following sections, we'll explore additional strategies for understanding your audience's needs, personalizing your content, and nurturing brand advocates to further deepen your connections with your followers.

2.4 Creating a Community Around Your Brand

A strong community surrounding your brand can have a significant impact on your social media success. By fostering a sense of belonging and connection among your followers, you can boost engagement, loyalty, and advocacy. In this section, we'll discuss strategies for creating and nurturing a community around your brand and how it can contribute to building authentic relationships with your audience.

1. Develop a brand mission and values: Clearly define your brand's mission and values, and communicate them consistently across your social media channels. This helps your audience understand your purpose and what you stand for, making it easier for them to connect with your brand on a deeper level.

2. Be authentic and transparent: Share your brand's story, successes, and challenges openly with your audience. Transparency fosters trust and allows your followers to feel more connected to your brand, making it easier for them to become part of your community.

3. Create a dedicated online space: Establish a dedicated space for your community to interact, such as a Facebook group, forum, or Slack channel. This provides your audience with a platform to share their experiences, ask questions, and engage with your brand and each other.

4. Encourage interaction and collaboration: Actively promote collaboration and interaction among your community members by hosting events, challenges, or discussions. Encourage your followers to share their thoughts, ideas, and experiences, and facilitate connections between them.

5. Provide value and support: Offer resources, information, and support to your community members to help them achieve their goals or overcome challenges. This could include educational content, expert advice, or access to exclusive tools and resources. By providing value, you can foster loyalty and strengthen your community.

6. Recognize and celebrate your community: Show appreciation for your community members by acknowledging and celebrating their achievements, contributions, and milestones. This can include featuring their stories on your social media channels, sending personalized messages, or offering rewards and incentives for their engagement.

7. Monitor and nurture: Regularly monitor the health and growth of your community, and address any issues or conflicts that may arise. Continue to nurture your community by providing valuable content, encouraging interaction, and fostering a positive and supportive environment.

By creating a community around your brand, you can build stronger, more authentic relationships with your audience and encourage long-term loyalty and advocacy. In the next section, we'll discuss the importance of understanding your audience's needs and personalizing your content to further strengthen your relationships with your followers.

2.5 Responding to Feedback and Criticism

Dealing with feedback and criticism is an inevitable part of maintaining a social media presence. How you handle negative comments or feedback can significantly impact your brand's reputation and relationships with your audience. In this section, we'll discuss strategies for responding to feedback and criticism in a constructive and professional manner that can help you build stronger connections with your followers.

1. Listen and acknowledge: When faced with negative feedback or criticism, start by listening carefully to the concerns or issues raised by the commenter. Acknowledge their feelings or frustrations, and thank them for taking the time to share their thoughts. This demonstrates that you're open to feedback and willing to learn from it.

2. Respond professionally and empathetically: Address the concerns or issues raised by the commenter in a professional and empathetic manner. Avoid becoming defensive or dismissive, and instead, focus on understanding the problem and providing a thoughtful response.

3. Offer solutions or assistance: If appropriate, offer a solution or assistance to the commenter to address their concerns or issues. This could include providing additional information, directing them to relevant resources, or offering a refund or replacement for

a faulty product.

4. Take the conversation offline: In some cases, it may be more appropriate to take the conversation offline by inviting the commenter to contact you directly via email or private message. This allows you to address their concerns or issues in a more personal and private manner.

5. Learn from the feedback: Use negative feedback and criticism as an opportunity to learn and improve your brand or content. Reflect on the comments and consider whether there are any valid points that you can address to enhance your social media presence and better serve your audience.

6. Monitor and address recurring issues: Keep an eye on your social media channels to identify any recurring themes or issues in the feedback you receive. If you notice a pattern, take action to address the underlying problem and prevent it from becoming a larger issue that could damage your brand's reputation.

By responding to feedback and criticism in a constructive and professional manner, you can demonstrate your commitment to your audience and foster stronger, more authentic relationships with your followers. In the following chapters, we'll continue to explore strategies for beating the algorithm, mastering each social media platform, and achieving exponential growth for your brand.

Chapter 3: Mastering the Art of Hashtags

Hashtags play a vital role in increasing the visibility of your content, reaching new audiences, and fostering engagement on social media platforms. By mastering the art of hashtags, you can optimize your content for discovery and better connect with your target audience. In this chapter, we'll delve into the science behind hashtags and discuss strategies for using them effectively to enhance your social media presence.

3.1 Decoding Hashtag Science

Understanding the science behind hashtags can help you make informed decisions about which ones to use, how many to include, and how to incorporate them into your content. Let's explore some key aspects of hashtag science to help you create a winning hashtag strategy.

1. Relevance: Use hashtags that are relevant to your content, audience, and industry. This increases the likelihood of your posts being discovered by users who are genuinely interested in your topic or niche, leading to more meaningful engagement.

2. Specificity: Opt for specific hashtags over generic ones. While generic hashtags, like #love or #instagood, may have a larger reach, they are also highly competitive and less likely to connect you with your target audience. Instead, use niche or industry-

specific hashtags to increase your chances of being discovered by users interested in your content.

3. Popularity: Consider the popularity of a hashtag before using it. Highly popular hashtags may get your content lost in the noise, while obscure hashtags may not have enough visibility to make an impact. Strike a balance by using a mix of popular and moderately popular hashtags to maximize your reach.

4. Hashtag research: Regularly research new and trending hashtags in your industry or niche. This can help you stay up-to-date with current trends and ensure that your content remains relevant and discoverable. Tools like Hashtagify or RiteTag can help you identify popular and relevant hashtags.

5. Quantity: Be mindful of the number of hashtags you use in your posts. While Instagram allows up to 30 hashtags per post, using too many can appear spammy and detract from your message. Experiment with different quantities to find the sweet spot for your brand and audience.

6. Placement: Consider where to place your hashtags in your post. You can include them within the caption, at the end of the caption, or in a comment on the post. Test different placements to determine what works best for your brand and audience.

By decoding hashtag science and incorporating these strategies into your social media content, you can enhance the visibility of your posts, reach new audiences, and foster engagement with your target audience. In the following sections, we'll explore additional hashtag strategies, such as creating branded hashtags and leveraging local and event-specific hashtags, to further amplify your social media presence.

3.2 Choosing the Right Hashtags for Your Content

Selecting the appropriate hashtags for your content is crucial for maximizing your reach and connecting with your target audience. In this section, we'll discuss strategies for choosing the right hashtags and tailoring them to your content and objectives.

1. Align with your content: Ensure that the hashtags you choose directly relate to the content of your post. This helps users find your content when searching for specific topics and increases the likelihood of meaningful engagement.

2. Analyze your competitors: Examine the hashtags used by your competitors and industry influencers to identify those that resonate with your target audience. While you don't want to copy their exact strategy, this research can help you discover popular hashtags and trends within your niche.

3. Utilize hashtag tools: Use hashtag research tools like Hashtagify, RiteTag, or Keyhole to find trending and relevant hashtags for your content. These tools can help you discover popular hashtags, analyze their performance, and suggest new ones based on your content.

4. Mix it up: Use a combination of popular, moderately popular, and niche-specific hashtags to maximize your reach and visibility. Popular hashtags can offer broad exposure, while niche-specific

hashtags can help you connect with a more targeted audience.

5. Create branded hashtags: Develop unique branded hashtags for your business or campaign to encourage user-generated content, track engagement, and create a sense of community around your brand. Encourage your followers to use your branded hashtags when sharing content related to your brand, products, or services.

6. Leverage local and event-specific hashtags: Take advantage of local and event-specific hashtags to connect with users in your area or those attending a particular event. This can help you tap into local conversations, increase your visibility, and attract new followers who are interested in your niche or location.

7. Test and evaluate: Regularly assess the performance of your hashtag strategy by tracking engagement, reach, and other relevant metrics. Use this data to identify which hashtags are driving the most engagement and adjust your strategy accordingly.

By choosing the right hashtags for your content and tailoring them to your audience and objectives, you can increase the visibility of your posts, connect with your target audience, and foster meaningful engagement. In the following sections, we'll delve deeper into hashtag best practices for specific social media platforms and how to adapt your strategy to each platform's unique features and requirements.

3.3 Balancing Broad and Niche Hashtags

Striking a balance between broad and niche hashtags is essential for maximizing the visibility and engagement of your social media content. Broad hashtags may offer a wider reach, while niche hashtags help you connect with a more targeted and engaged audience. In this section, we'll discuss strategies for balancing the use of broad and niche hashtags in your social media posts.

1. Identify your objectives: Start by clarifying your goals for each post, whether it's to reach a larger audience, increase engagement, or drive traffic to your website. This will help you determine the appropriate mix of broad and niche hashtags for each piece of content.

2. Start with broad hashtags: Begin by including a few popular or broad hashtags in your post to increase its visibility to a wider audience. While these hashtags may be more competitive, they can help boost your overall reach and potentially attract new followers.

3. Incorporate niche hashtags: After including a few broad hashtags, add niche or industry-specific hashtags to target a more relevant and engaged audience. These hashtags are less competitive and can help you connect with users who are genuinely interested in your content or industry.

4. Research your target audience: Understand the hashtags your target audience is using and engaging with. This can help you identify niche hashtags that resonate with your audience and increase the likelihood of meaningful engagement.

5. Use a mix of hashtag lengths: Combine short, medium, and long hashtags to maximize your chances of being discovered by users with different search habits. Shorter hashtags may be more popular and competitive, while longer, more specific hashtags can help you reach a more targeted audience.

6. Experiment and analyze: Continuously experiment with different combinations of broad and niche hashtags to find the optimal balance for your content and objectives. Monitor the performance of your hashtags in terms of reach, engagement, and other relevant metrics, and adjust your strategy based on your findings.

By balancing broad and niche hashtags in your social media content, you can increase your visibility, connect with your target audience, and foster meaningful engagement. In the following sections, we'll explore hashtag best practices for specific social media platforms and discuss how to adapt your hashtag strategy to each platform's unique features and requirements.

3.4 Tracking Hashtag Performance

Monitoring and analyzing the performance of your hashtags is crucial for optimizing your social media strategy and achieving your desired results. By tracking hashtag performance, you can identify which hashtags are driving the most engagement and adjust your approach accordingly. In this section, we'll discuss strategies for tracking hashtag performance and using this data to inform your social media strategy.

1. Define your key performance indicators (KPIs): Start by identifying the KPIs that align with your social media objectives, such as reach, engagement, click-through rate, or conversions. This will help you determine which metrics to track and how to measure the success of your hashtag strategy.

2. Use analytics tools: Leverage social media analytics tools like Hootsuite, Sprout Social, or native platform analytics (e.g., Instagram Insights) to track the performance of your hashtags. These tools can provide valuable data on the reach, impressions, engagement, and other metrics associated with your hashtags.

3. Monitor user-generated content: Keep an eye on user-generated content that includes your branded or campaign-specific hashtags. This can help you gauge the effectiveness of your hashtags in encouraging user participation and generating buzz around your brand or campaign.

4. Analyze hashtag trends: Regularly analyze hashtag trends within your industry or niche to identify popular and emerging hashtags. This can help you stay up-to-date with current trends and ensure that your content remains relevant and discoverable.

5. Conduct A/B testing: Experiment with different combinations of hashtags to determine which ones drive the most engagement and conversions. By conducting A/B tests, you can identify the optimal mix of hashtags for your content and objectives.

6. Adjust your strategy: Based on your hashtag performance data, adjust your social media strategy to incorporate the most effective hashtags and tactics. Continuously refine your approach to stay ahead of trends and maximize your reach and engagement.

By tracking hashtag performance and using this data to inform your social media strategy, you can optimize your content for discovery, reach, and engagement. In the next sections, we'll delve into hashtag best practices for specific social media platforms and discuss how to adapt your hashtag strategy to each platform's unique features and requirements.

3.5 Creating Branded Hashtags

Branded hashtags are unique to your business, campaign, or event and can help you track engagement, encourage user-generated content, and create a sense of community around your brand. In this section, we'll discuss strategies for creating effective branded hashtags and incorporating them into your social media strategy.

1. Keep it simple and memorable: Your branded hashtag should be easy to remember and spell, so users can quickly recall and use it in their posts. Aim for a concise and catchy hashtag that reflects your brand identity and message.

2. Make it unique: Ensure your branded hashtag is unique to your brand or campaign to avoid confusion with other hashtags or competitors. Research existing hashtags to verify that your chosen hashtag is not already being used for a different purpose.

3. Promote your branded hashtag: Integrate your branded hashtag into your social media content, website, email marketing, and other promotional materials to encourage users to adopt and use it in their posts. This will help you increase the visibility of your hashtag and foster user-generated content.

4. Encourage user-generated content: Motivate your followers to use your branded hashtag when sharing content related to your brand, products, or services. You can do this by hosting contests,

featuring user-generated content on your social media channels, or offering incentives for using your branded hashtag.

5. Monitor and engage with users: Regularly monitor your branded hashtag to track its performance, identify user-generated content, and engage with users who are using your hashtag. This can help you build relationships with your followers and create a sense of community around your brand.

6. Measure the impact: Use social media analytics tools to measure the impact of your branded hashtag on your reach, engagement, and other relevant metrics. This data can help you assess the effectiveness of your branded hashtag strategy and make adjustments as needed.

By creating and effectively promoting your branded hashtags, you can foster user-generated content, track engagement, and cultivate a sense of community around your brand. In the following sections, we'll explore hashtag best practices for specific social media platforms and discuss how to adapt your hashtag strategy to each platform's unique features and requirements.

Chapter 4: Driving Growth with Analytics

Harnessing the power of analytics is essential for understanding the effectiveness of your social media strategy and making data-driven decisions to drive growth. By analyzing key performance indicators (KPIs), you can identify areas for improvement and optimize your content, engagement, and overall social media presence. In this chapter, we'll discuss strategies for analyzing KPIs and using this data to inform your social media strategy.

4.1 Analyzing Key Performance Indicators

KPIs are quantifiable metrics that help you measure the success of your social media efforts in relation to your objectives. By closely analyzing these indicators, you can gain valuable insights into your social media performance and make informed decisions to drive growth. Here are some strategies for analyzing KPIs effectively:

1. Set clear objectives: Begin by defining your social media objectives, such as increasing brand awareness, driving website traffic, or generating leads. This will help you determine which KPIs are most relevant to your goals and provide a benchmark for measuring success.

2. Select relevant KPIs: Choose KPIs that align with your objectives and provide actionable insights into your social media

performance. Some common KPIs include reach, impressions, engagement, click-through rate, conversions, and return on investment (ROI).

3. Use analytics tools: Leverage social media analytics tools like Hootsuite, Sprout Social, or native platform analytics (e.g., Facebook Insights, Instagram Insights) to collect and analyze data on your KPIs. These tools can help you track your performance over time, identify trends, and gain insights into your audience demographics and behavior.

4. Monitor your KPIs regularly: Regularly review your KPI data to identify patterns, trends, and areas for improvement. This can help you optimize your content, engagement tactics, and overall social media strategy for better results.

5. Conduct A/B testing: Experiment with different content types, posting times, and engagement tactics to determine which approaches yield the best results in terms of your KPIs. Use A/B testing to compare the performance of different strategies and identify the most effective methods for achieving your objectives.

6. Analyze competitor performance: Assess the KPIs of your competitors and industry influencers to gain insights into their social media strategies and identify opportunities for improvement. This can help you stay ahead of the competition and refine your approach for better results.

7. Adjust your strategy: Use your KPI analysis to inform your social media strategy and make data-driven decisions for growth. Continuously refine your approach based on your findings to maximize your reach, engagement, and overall performance.

By analyzing key performance indicators and using this data to inform your social media strategy, you can optimize your content, engagement, and overall presence for growth. In the following sections, we'll delve deeper into the use of analytics for specific social media platforms and discuss how to adapt your analytics strategy to each platform's unique features and requirements.

4.2 Interpreting Audience Insights

Understanding your audience is crucial for creating content that resonates with them and drives engagement. By interpreting audience insights from your social media analytics, you can gain valuable information about your followers' demographics, interests, and behaviors. In this section, we'll discuss strategies for interpreting audience insights and using this data to inform your social media strategy.

1. Review demographic data: Analyze demographic information about your audience, such as age, gender, location, and language. This data can help you create content that appeals to your target audience and tailor your messaging to resonate with them.

2. Assess interests and preferences: Examine your audience's interests, preferences, and online behaviors to gain insights into their content consumption habits. This can help you identify topics and formats that are likely to engage your followers and drive meaningful interactions.

3. Identify influencers and brand advocates: Determine who your most engaged followers are and which users have the most significant influence within your niche. This can help you identify potential collaboration partners, brand advocates, and influencers who can help amplify your message and grow your audience.

4. Analyze content performance: Assess which types of content perform best with your audience in terms of reach, engagement, and other relevant metrics. Use this data to inform your content strategy and prioritize the creation of content that resonates with your followers.

5. Monitor audience sentiment: Analyze the sentiment of your audience's interactions with your content, such as comments, likes, and shares. This can help you gauge your audience's overall satisfaction with your content and identify any areas for improvement.

6. Evaluate audience growth and attrition: Track the growth of your audience over time, as well as any fluctuations in follower count. This can help you identify patterns and trends in your audience growth, as well as any factors that may contribute to follower attrition.

7. Leverage audience insights for content creation: Use the insights gained from your audience analysis to create content that appeals to their interests, preferences, and needs. This will help you establish a stronger connection with your audience and drive engagement on your social media channels.

By interpreting audience insights and using this data to inform your social media strategy, you can create content that resonates with your followers and drives meaningful engagement. In the following sections, we'll explore analytics best practices for specific social media platforms and discuss how to adapt your analytics strategy to each platform's unique features and requirements.

4.3 Adjusting Your Strategy Based on Data

Using data-driven insights to adjust your social media strategy is essential for maximizing your reach, engagement, and overall performance. By analyzing your analytics data, you can identify areas for improvement and make informed decisions to drive growth. In this section, we'll discuss strategies for adjusting your social media strategy based on data.

1. Identify areas for improvement: Analyze your analytics data to pinpoint areas where your social media performance is falling short of your objectives. This may include content that receives low engagement, posting times that result in limited reach, or ineffective engagement tactics.

2. Test new approaches: Experiment with new content types, formats, posting times, and engagement tactics to determine which methods yield the best results. Use A/B testing to compare the performance of different strategies and identify the most effective approaches for achieving your objectives.

3. Monitor the impact of changes: Continuously monitor the performance of your adjusted strategies to determine their effectiveness in driving growth. Keep an eye on key performance indicators (KPIs) to assess the impact of your changes and make further adjustments as needed.

4. Learn from your competitors: Evaluate your competitors' social media strategies and performance to identify successful tactics and areas for improvement. Use this information to adjust your own strategy and stay ahead of the competition.

5. Stay current with industry trends: Keep up-to-date with the latest trends and best practices in social media marketing to ensure your strategy remains relevant and effective. Regularly adjust your approach to align with evolving platform features, user behaviors, and industry developments.

6. Leverage audience insights: Use the audience insights gathered from your analytics data to create content that appeals to your followers' interests, preferences, and needs. Continuously refine your content strategy based on these insights to foster deeper connections with your audience and drive engagement.

7. Measure and refine ROI: Assess the return on investment (ROI) of your social media efforts to ensure you're allocating resources effectively. Adjust your strategy to focus on the tactics that deliver the highest ROI and align with your overall business objectives.

By adjusting your social media strategy based on data-driven insights, you can optimize your content, engagement tactics, and overall presence for growth. In the following sections, we'll delve deeper into the use of analytics for specific social media platforms and discuss how to adapt your analytics strategy to each platform's unique features and requirements.

4.4 A/B Testing for Maximum Impact

A/B testing, also known as split testing, is a powerful tool for optimizing your social media strategy by comparing the performance of two or more variations of your content, engagement tactics, or other elements. By conducting A/B tests, you can identify the most effective methods for achieving your objectives and make data-driven decisions to drive growth. In this section, we'll discuss strategies for conducting A/B tests and using the results to inform your social media strategy.

1. Define your objectives: Begin by identifying the objectives of your A/B test, such as increasing engagement, improving click-through rate, or boosting conversions. This will help you determine which elements to test and establish a benchmark for measuring success.

2. Choose the elements to test: Select the variables you want to test, such as content types, headlines, images, hashtags, posting times, or engagement tactics. Focus on elements that have a direct impact on your objectives and can be easily modified.

3. Create test variations: Develop two or more variations of the element you're testing, ensuring that all other aspects of your content or strategy remain consistent. This will allow you to isolate the impact of the variable being tested and accurately measure its effect on performance.

4. Run your test: Share your test variations with your audience, either simultaneously or sequentially, depending on the nature of your test. Be sure to gather a sufficient amount of data to make statistically significant comparisons between the variations.

5. Analyze the results: Compare the performance of your test variations based on key performance indicators (KPIs) that align with your objectives. Evaluate the differences in performance to determine which variation is most effective in achieving your goals.

6. Implement the winning variation: Apply the insights gained from your A/B test to your social media strategy by implementing the winning variation in your content, engagement tactics, or other elements. Monitor the impact of this change on your performance to ensure it delivers the expected results.

7. Continuously test and optimize: Conduct regular A/B tests to identify opportunities for improvement and continuously optimize your social media strategy for growth. Experiment with different elements and combinations to uncover the most effective methods for achieving your objectives.

By leveraging A/B testing to inform your social media strategy, you can optimize your content, engagement tactics, and overall presence for maximum impact. In the following sections, we'll explore analytics best practices for specific social media platforms and discuss how to adapt your analytics strategy to each platform's unique features and requirements.

4.5 Leveraging Social Media Management Tools

Social media management tools can greatly enhance your ability to analyze data, conduct A/B tests, schedule posts, and engage with your audience. By leveraging these tools, you can streamline your social media strategy and make data-driven decisions to drive growth. In this section, we'll discuss strategies for effectively using social media management tools to inform your social media strategy.

1. Choose the right tool: Select a social media management tool that aligns with your needs, objectives, and budget. Popular options include Hootsuite, Sprout Social, and Buffer. Consider factors such as ease of use, analytics capabilities, and integration with your preferred social media platforms.

2. Centralize your social media accounts: Connect all of your social media accounts to your chosen management tool to streamline your content creation, scheduling, and analytics efforts. This will help you maintain a consistent presence across platforms and simplify your workflow.

3. Schedule your content: Use your social media management tool to schedule your content in advance, freeing up time to focus on engagement and other strategic activities. Experiment with different posting times and frequencies to identify the optimal schedule for your audience.

4. Monitor and engage with your audience: Leverage your management tool's engagement features to track mentions, comments, and messages across your social media accounts. Respond to your audience in a timely manner to foster relationships and build a sense of community around your brand.

5. Conduct A/B tests: Utilize your social media management tool's A/B testing capabilities to experiment with different content types, headlines, images, hashtags, and other elements. Analyze the results to identify the most effective strategies for achieving your objectives.

6. Analyze your performance: Use your management tool's analytics features to track key performance indicators (KPIs), evaluate the success of your content and engagement tactics, and identify areas for improvement. Adjust your strategy based on these insights to drive growth.

7. Optimize for each platform: Leverage platform-specific features and analytics within your social media management tool to optimize your strategy for each social media platform. Tailor your content, engagement tactics, and analytics approach to the unique requirements and audience behaviors of each platform.

By leveraging social media management tools to inform your social media strategy, you can streamline your workflow, optimize your content and engagement tactics, and make data-driven decisions to drive growth. In the following sections, we'll delve deeper into the use of analytics for specific social media platforms and discuss how to adapt your analytics strategy to each platform's unique features and requirements.

Chapter 5: Platform-Specific Tips and Tricks

5.1 Mastering Instagram's Algorithm

Instagram is a highly visual platform that places a strong emphasis on user engagement and content relevance. By understanding and working with Instagram's algorithm, you can increase the visibility of your content and grow your audience. In this section, we'll discuss strategies for mastering Instagram's algorithm and optimizing your presence on the platform.

1. Prioritize high-quality visuals: Instagram is a visual platform, and high-quality images and videos are crucial for capturing your audience's attention. Invest time and effort into creating visually appealing content that reflects your brand identity and resonates with your audience.

2. Engage with your audience: Respond to comments, like and share user-generated content, and participate in conversations to foster relationships with your followers. This can help improve the visibility of your content in the algorithm and create a loyal, engaged audience.

3. Post consistently: Maintain a consistent posting schedule to keep your content fresh and visible in your followers' feeds. Experiment with different posting times and frequencies to determine the optimal schedule for your audience.

4. Use relevant hashtags: Incorporate relevant and targeted hashtags in your captions to increase the discoverability of your content. Balance the use of popular hashtags with niche hashtags to reach a broader audience while maintaining relevance to your target demographic.

5. Leverage Instagram Stories and Reels: Take advantage of Instagram's various content formats, such as Stories and Reels, to increase your content's reach and engagement. These formats can help your content stand out in the algorithm and attract new followers.

6. Collaborate with influencers and partners: Partner with influencers, brands, and other creators in your niche to expand your reach and tap into new audiences. This can help improve your content's visibility in the algorithm and drive growth.

7. Monitor your analytics: Regularly analyze your Instagram insights to track the performance of your content, identify trends and patterns, and adjust your strategy accordingly. Focus on key performance indicators (KPIs) such as reach, engagement, and follower growth.

8. Experiment with Instagram ads: Utilize Instagram's advertising platform to promote your content and reach a larger, targeted audience. This can help boost your visibility in the algorithm and

drive growth.

By mastering Instagram's algorithm and implementing these strategies, you can optimize your presence on the platform and drive meaningful engagement with your audience. In the following sections, we'll explore platform-specific tips and tricks for other popular social media platforms and discuss how to adapt your strategy to each platform's unique features and requirements.

5.2 Winning the Facebook Game

Facebook remains a dominant player in the social media landscape, offering a wide range of features and tools for businesses and creators to connect with their audience. By understanding and optimizing your approach to Facebook's algorithm, you can boost your content's visibility and grow your audience. In this section, we'll discuss strategies for winning the Facebook game and maximizing your presence on the platform.

1. Prioritize meaningful engagement: Facebook's algorithm favors content that generates meaningful interactions, such as comments, shares, and reactions. Encourage conversations and discussions in your posts by asking questions, sharing opinions, and engaging with your audience's comments.

2. Create shareable content: Craft content that is likely to be shared by your audience, such as informative articles, entertaining videos, or relatable memes. Shares can significantly improve your content's reach and visibility in the Facebook algorithm.

3. Utilize Facebook Live: Engage your audience in real-time with Facebook Live broadcasts. Live videos often receive higher levels of engagement and can help improve your content's visibility in the algorithm.

4. Post consistently: Maintain a consistent posting schedule to ensure your content remains fresh and visible in your followers' newsfeeds. Experiment with different posting times and frequencies to find the optimal schedule for your audience.

5. Leverage Facebook Groups: Participate in or create Facebook Groups related to your niche to connect with like-minded

individuals and share your content. This can help expand your reach and improve your content's visibility in the algorithm.

6. Optimize your content for mobile: As a significant portion of Facebook users access the platform via mobile devices, it's crucial to optimize your content for mobile viewing. Ensure your images, videos, and text are easily viewable and engaging on smaller screens.

7. Monitor your analytics: Use Facebook Insights to track the performance of your content, identify trends and patterns, and adjust your strategy accordingly. Focus on key performance indicators (KPIs) such as reach, engagement, and page likes.

8. Experiment with Facebook ads: Leverage Facebook's advertising platform to promote your content and reach a larger, targeted audience. This can help boost your visibility in the algorithm and drive growth.

By implementing these strategies and optimizing your approach to Facebook's algorithm, you can maximize your presence on the platform and drive meaningful engagement with your audience. In the following sections, we'll explore platform-specific tips and tricks for other popular social media platforms and discuss how to adapt your strategy to each platform's unique features and requirements.

5.3 Conquering Twitter's Fast-Paced Landscape

Twitter's fast-paced nature and character limits present unique challenges and opportunities for businesses and creators seeking to connect with their audience. By understanding and adapting to Twitter's algorithm and user behavior, you can increase the visibility of your content and grow your following. In this section, we'll discuss strategies for conquering Twitter's fast-paced landscape and optimizing your presence on the platform.

1. Craft concise, engaging tweets: Twitter's character limit forces you to be concise and creative with your content. Write clear, engaging tweets that capture your audience's attention and encourage retweets, replies, and likes.

2. Utilize hashtags effectively: Incorporate relevant and targeted hashtags in your tweets to increase their discoverability and reach a broader audience. Balance the use of popular hashtags with niche hashtags to maintain relevance to your target demographic.

3. Engage in real-time conversations: Twitter is an ideal platform for real-time engagement and conversation. Participate in trending topics, events, and discussions related to your niche to connect with your audience and increase your content's visibility.

4. Post frequently and consistently: Due to Twitter's fast-paced nature, posting frequently and consistently is essential to maintaining visibility in your followers' timelines. Experiment with different posting times and frequencies to find the optimal schedule for your audience.

5. Leverage Twitter's multimedia features: Enhance your tweets with images, videos, and GIFs to capture your audience's attention and drive engagement. Utilize Twitter's multimedia features, such

as Twitter Fleets and Twitter Spaces, to diversify your content and reach new audiences.

6. Utilize mentions and retweets: Mention and engage with influencers, brands, and other users in your niche to expand your reach and tap into new audiences. Retweet relevant content from other users to curate valuable content for your followers and foster relationships.

7. Monitor your analytics: Use Twitter Analytics to track the performance of your tweets, identify trends and patterns, and adjust your strategy accordingly. Focus on key performance indicators (KPIs) such as impressions, engagement, and follower growth.

8. Experiment with Twitter ads: Leverage Twitter's advertising platform to promote your content and reach a larger, targeted audience. This can help boost your visibility in the algorithm and drive growth.

By implementing these strategies and optimizing your approach to Twitter's fast-paced landscape, you can maximize your presence on the platform and drive meaningful engagement with your audience. In the following sections, we'll explore platform-specific tips and tricks for other popular social media platforms and discuss how to adapt your strategy to each platform's unique features and requirements.

5.4 Capitalizing on LinkedIn's Professional Network

LinkedIn offers a unique opportunity to connect with a professional audience and establish your expertise within your niche. By understanding and leveraging LinkedIn's features and algorithm, you can increase the visibility of your content and grow your professional network. In this section, we'll discuss strategies for capitalizing on LinkedIn's professional network and optimizing your presence on the platform.

1. Optimize your profile: Ensure your LinkedIn profile is complete, up-to-date, and professional. Include a high-quality profile picture, compelling headline, detailed work experience, and relevant skills to showcase your expertise and credibility.

2. Share valuable content: Publish informative articles, thought-provoking insights, and industry news to demonstrate your expertise and provide value to your audience. Focus on creating content that resonates with your target demographic and encourages engagement.

3. Engage with your network: Interact with your connections by liking, commenting, and sharing their content. Engage in discussions and offer your insights to foster relationships and increase the visibility of your content in the LinkedIn algorithm.

4. Utilize LinkedIn Groups: Participate in or create LinkedIn Groups related to your niche to connect with like-minded professionals and share your content. This can help expand your reach and improve your content's visibility in the algorithm.

5. Leverage LinkedIn's multimedia features: Enhance your posts with images, videos, and presentations to capture your audience's attention and drive engagement. Utilize LinkedIn's multimedia

features, such as LinkedIn Live and LinkedIn Polls, to diversify your content and reach new audiences.

6. Post consistently: Maintain a consistent posting schedule to ensure your content remains fresh and visible in your followers' feeds. Experiment with different posting times and frequencies to find the optimal schedule for your audience.

7. Network strategically: Connect with professionals in your industry, potential clients, and influencers to expand your network and increase the visibility of your content. Be strategic in your networking efforts to ensure you're building a valuable and relevant professional network.

8. Monitor your analytics: Use LinkedIn Analytics to track the performance of your content, identify trends and patterns, and adjust your strategy accordingly. Focus on key performance indicators (KPIs) such as impressions, engagement, and connection growth.

9. Experiment with LinkedIn ads: Leverage LinkedIn's advertising platform to promote your content and reach a larger, targeted audience. This can help boost your visibility in the algorithm and drive growth.

By implementing these strategies and optimizing your approach to LinkedIn's professional network, you can maximize your presence on the platform and drive meaningful engagement with your audience. In the following sections, we'll explore platform-specific tips and tricks for other popular social media platforms and discuss how to adapt your strategy to each platform's unique features and requirements.

5.5 Exploring Emerging Platforms

Staying ahead of the curve in the ever-evolving social media landscape requires staying informed about emerging platforms and adapting your strategy accordingly. New platforms offer unique opportunities to connect with your audience, experiment with different content formats, and establish a strong presence before they become saturated. In this section, we'll discuss strategies for exploring emerging platforms and capitalizing on their potential for growth.

1. Stay informed: Keep an eye on industry news, trends, and reports to stay updated on the latest social media platforms and features. Regularly research new platforms and evaluate their potential for growth and relevance to your target audience.

2. Experiment with new formats: Emerging platforms often introduce new content formats and features. Embrace these new formats by experimenting with different types of content and evaluating their effectiveness in engaging your audience.

3. Be an early adopter: Establishing a presence on emerging platforms early on can give you a competitive advantage and enable you to build a following before the platform becomes saturated. Invest time and effort into building a strong presence on promising platforms to stay ahead of your competition.

4. Adapt your strategy: Each social media platform has unique features, user behaviors, and algorithms. Adapt your content strategy to cater to the specific requirements of each platform and maximize your content's reach and engagement.

5. Diversify your content portfolio: Utilize a diverse range of platforms and content formats to reach a broader audience and

cater to their varying preferences. Diversifying your content portfolio can help you stay relevant and ensure long-term growth.

6. Collaborate with early adopters: Partner with influencers, brands, and other creators who are early adopters of emerging platforms to tap into their audience and expand your reach. Collaborations can help improve your content's visibility and drive growth.

7. Monitor your analytics: Regularly analyze the performance of your content on emerging platforms to identify trends, patterns, and areas for improvement. Focus on key performance indicators (KPIs) such as reach, engagement, and follower growth.

8. Be prepared for change: The social media landscape is constantly evolving, and platforms may come and go. Be prepared to adapt your strategy and shift your focus as needed to capitalize on new opportunities and stay relevant.

By exploring emerging platforms and implementing these strategies, you can capitalize on their potential for growth and stay ahead in the ever-evolving social media landscape. In the following chapters, we'll delve deeper into specific strategies for growing your audience, optimizing your content, and mastering the art of social media.

Chapter 6: Captivating Content through Video

6.1 Embracing the Power of Video

In today's digital landscape, video has become an essential tool for captivating audiences and driving engagement on social media. With platforms like YouTube, TikTok, Instagram, and Facebook putting a strong emphasis on video content, businesses and creators must embrace the power of video to stay relevant and grow their online presence. In this section, we'll discuss the importance of video in your social media strategy and offer tips for creating compelling video content.

1. Understand the impact of video: Video content allows you to communicate your message in an engaging and easily digestible format. Studies show that viewers retain 95% of a message when they watch it in a video compared to 10% when reading it in text. Furthermore, video content generates higher engagement rates, including likes, comments, and shares, than other content formats.

2. Cater to different platforms: Different platforms have unique features and user behaviors that affect the optimal video format and length. Adapt your video content to cater to the specific requirements of each platform, such as short-form videos on TikTok and Instagram Reels or long-form content on YouTube.

3. Plan your content: Plan your video content by creating a storyboard, script, or outline before shooting. This will help ensure your message is clear and concise while maintaining a logical flow and structure.

4. Invest in quality: While the quality of your video doesn't have to

be on par with professional production, it's essential to maintain a minimum standard to keep your audience engaged. Invest in basic equipment, such as a decent camera, tripod, and microphone, and learn basic video editing skills to create visually appealing content.

5. Tell a story: Storytelling is a powerful tool for capturing your audience's attention and evoking an emotional response. Structure your video content around a narrative, whether it's an informative tutorial, a product review, or a personal anecdote, to keep your viewers engaged and entertained.

6. Incorporate visuals and sound: Enhance your video content with relevant visuals, such as text overlays, graphics, or animations, to reinforce your message and maintain viewer interest. Additionally, use background music or sound effects to create a more immersive and engaging experience.

7. Optimize for mobile: As a significant portion of social media users access platforms via mobile devices, it's crucial to optimize your video content for mobile viewing. Ensure your videos are easily viewable and engaging on smaller screens, and consider creating vertical videos for platforms like Instagram and TikTok.

8. Monitor your analytics: Track the performance of your video content using platform-specific analytics tools to identify trends, patterns, and areas for improvement. Focus on key performance indicators (KPIs) such as views, watch time, and engagement.

By embracing the power of video and implementing these tips, you can create captivating content that drives engagement and helps you grow your audience on social media. In the following sections, we'll explore more strategies for optimizing your video content and leveraging the unique features of different platforms.

6.2 Understanding Video Formats and Platforms

Each social media platform has its own unique features, user behaviors, and optimal video formats. Understanding the differences between platforms and the types of video content that perform best on each can help you tailor your strategy and maximize your reach and engagement. In this section, we'll discuss the key aspects of various video formats and platforms, and offer tips for optimizing your content accordingly.

1. YouTube: As the largest video-sharing platform, YouTube is ideal for long-form content, such as tutorials, vlogs, product reviews, and interviews. Optimize your YouTube videos by creating eye-catching thumbnails, writing SEO-friendly titles and descriptions, and utilizing relevant tags. Engage with your audience through the comment section and encourage viewers to like, share, and subscribe to your channel.

2. Instagram: Instagram offers multiple video formats, including Instagram Stories, IGTV, and Reels. Stories are perfect for short, ephemeral content that disappears after 24 hours, while IGTV allows you to create longer, more in-depth videos. Reels, on the other hand, are ideal for short, engaging clips set to music. Ensure your Instagram videos are visually appealing and attention-grabbing to stand out in users' feeds and the Explore page.

3. TikTok: TikTok is a short-form video platform that focuses on engaging, creative content set to music. Create entertaining and shareable TikTok videos by participating in challenges, trends, and memes, while showcasing your brand's personality. Use relevant hashtags and experiment with the platform's various editing features and effects to enhance your content.

4. Facebook: Facebook supports various video formats, including short-form clips, live videos, and Facebook Watch for longer

content. Tailor your Facebook video strategy to your audience's preferences, and utilize features like captions, reactions, and comments to drive engagement. Consider using Facebook Live to broadcast events, Q&A sessions, or behind-the-scenes content to connect with your followers in real-time.

5. Twitter: Twitter's short video format is ideal for sharing quick updates, teasers, or engaging snippets from longer content. Optimize your Twitter videos by keeping them concise, engaging, and shareable. Utilize captions to make your content accessible and to capture the attention of users scrolling through their feeds.

6. LinkedIn: LinkedIn is a professional networking platform where informative and industry-related video content performs well. Share thought leadership pieces, company updates, and relevant industry news to engage your professional audience. Optimize your LinkedIn videos by keeping them concise and professional, and accompany them with a well-written description and relevant hashtags.

By understanding the unique features and optimal video formats of each platform, you can tailor your content strategy to maximize reach, engagement, and growth. In the following sections, we'll explore more strategies for creating compelling video content and leveraging the power of video to grow your social media presence.

6.3 Creating Engaging Video Concepts

A key aspect of captivating your audience with video content is developing engaging concepts that resonate with your target audience and align with your brand's identity. In this section, we'll discuss strategies for brainstorming and creating compelling video concepts that drive engagement and help you grow your social media presence.

1. Identify your audience's interests: Research your target audience to understand their preferences, challenges, and interests. Analyze your existing content to determine which topics and formats perform best, and use this information to inform your video concepts.

2. Align with your brand identity: Ensure your video content aligns with your brand's identity, values, and messaging. This consistency helps to establish your brand's unique voice and solidify your audience's connection with your content.

3. Monitor trends and viral content: Keep an eye on current trends, viral content, and popular challenges within your niche and on each platform. Incorporating these trends into your video concepts can help increase your content's visibility and appeal to your target audience.

4. Address your audience's pain points: Create content that addresses your audience's challenges, concerns, or problems. Offer solutions, insights, and advice to demonstrate your expertise and provide value to your viewers.

5. Utilize storytelling techniques: Engage your audience by structuring your video content around a narrative, whether it's a tutorial, a case study, or a behind-the-scenes look at your

business. Storytelling helps maintain viewer interest and create an emotional connection with your content.

6. Experiment with different formats: Diversify your content by experimenting with various video formats, such as interviews, live streams, animations, and documentaries. This variety keeps your audience engaged and caters to different preferences and interests.

7. Leverage user-generated content: Encourage your audience to create and share their own video content related to your brand or niche. User-generated content can help build a sense of community and provide new ideas for your own video concepts.

8. Collaborate with influencers and other creators: Partner with influencers or other creators within your niche to create engaging, shareable video content. Collaborations can help expand your reach, introduce your content to new audiences, and provide fresh perspectives for your video concepts.

9. Analyze your competition: Study the video content of your competitors and identify what works well for them. Use this information to inspire your own video concepts and find unique ways to differentiate your content from the competition.

By implementing these strategies, you can develop engaging video concepts that resonate with your target audience and drive growth on your social media platforms. In the following sections, we'll delve deeper into strategies for optimizing your video content and leveraging the unique features of different platforms to maximize your reach and engagement.

6.4 Editing Techniques for Maximum Impact

Effective video editing can significantly enhance the overall impact and appeal of your content. By utilizing various editing techniques, you can create professional, engaging videos that capture your audience's attention and drive engagement. In this section, we'll discuss editing techniques that can help you maximize the impact of your video content on social media.

1. Use jump cuts: Jump cuts help maintain a fast pace and keep your audience engaged by eliminating unnecessary pauses or repetitive content. Be mindful not to overuse jump cuts, as they can be jarring if used excessively.

2. Add text overlays: Use text overlays to emphasize key points, provide additional information, or make your video content more accessible to viewers watching without sound. Ensure the text is legible and visually appealing, and consider using animations or effects to enhance its impact.

3. Incorporate B-roll footage: B-roll footage consists of supplementary video clips that help to illustrate or support the main content. Utilize B-roll to add visual interest, provide context, and enhance the overall storytelling of your video.

4. Utilize transitions: Smooth transitions between clips can improve the flow of your video and create a more polished, professional look. Experiment with different transition styles, such as crossfades, wipes, or slides, to find the ones that best suit your content and aesthetic.

5. Enhance with music and sound effects: Background music and sound effects can create a more immersive and engaging experience for your viewers. Choose music that aligns with your

brand's identity and the mood of your video, and use sound effects sparingly to emphasize key moments or create a specific atmosphere.

6. Optimize for mobile viewing: Ensure your video content is easily viewable and engaging on smaller screens by keeping text and graphics large enough to read and maintaining a clean, uncluttered visual composition.

7. Adjust color grading and filters: Color grading and filters can significantly impact the overall look and feel of your video content. Experiment with different color grading techniques and filters to create a consistent aesthetic that aligns with your brand's identity.

8. Use graphics and animations: Graphics and animations can add visual interest, reinforce your message, and create a more engaging viewing experience. Incorporate graphics and animations to illustrate key points, introduce new sections, or add a touch of creativity to your content.

9. Edit for pacing: Keep your audience engaged by maintaining a consistent pace throughout your video. Remove any unnecessary pauses or lengthy segments, and consider using a mix of short and long clips to maintain viewer interest.

10. Review and refine: Before publishing your video, watch it multiple times to ensure it flows smoothly and effectively communicates your message. Make any necessary adjustments to the editing, pacing, or visuals to create the most impactful content possible.

By implementing these editing techniques, you can create professional, engaging video content that captivates your audience and maximizes your social media growth. In the following sections, we'll explore more strategies for optimizing your video content and leveraging the unique features of different platforms to expand your reach and drive engagement.

6.5 Live Streaming for Real-Time Connection

Live streaming has become an increasingly popular format for connecting with your audience in real-time, fostering engagement, and providing unique, interactive experiences. By incorporating live streaming into your social media strategy, you can build stronger relationships with your followers, offer exclusive content, and boost your overall online presence. In this section, we'll discuss strategies for leveraging live streaming to create real-time connections with your audience.

1. Choose the right platform: Different social media platforms offer live streaming features, such as Instagram Live, Facebook Live, YouTube Live, and LinkedIn Live. Choose the platform that best suits your audience's preferences and your content goals, and familiarize yourself with the platform's features and best practices.

2. Plan your content: While live streaming allows for spontaneity, it's essential to plan your content to ensure a smooth, engaging broadcast. Outline the main points you want to cover, prepare any visual aids or props, and rehearse your presentation to build confidence and minimize technical issues.

3. Promote your live stream: Announce your live stream in advance to give your audience time to plan their attendance. Share teasers, reminders, and countdowns on your social media channels, and consider sending out email invitations or push notifications to maximize your reach.

4. Engage with your audience: One of the main benefits of live streaming is the opportunity for real-time interaction with your viewers. Encourage questions and comments, respond to feedback, and acknowledge your audience members by name to foster a sense of connection and community.

5. Offer exclusive content: Utilize live streaming to provide your audience with unique content, such as behind-the-scenes tours, product launches, live tutorials, or Q&A sessions. Exclusive content can help incentivize viewers to attend your live stream and drive engagement.

6. Collaborate with guests and influencers: Invite guests, industry experts, or influencers to join your live stream, offering fresh perspectives and expanding your reach to new audiences. Plan your collaboration ahead of time to ensure a smooth, engaging experience for your viewers.

7. Monitor and moderate comments: Assign a team member to monitor and moderate the comments during your live stream, addressing any inappropriate behavior, and highlighting relevant questions or feedback for you to respond to.

8. Repurpose your live stream: After your live stream has ended, repurpose the content by uploading it to your social media channels or converting it into a blog post, podcast episode, or video series. This helps to maximize your content's value and reach.

9. Analyze performance: Review the performance of your live stream, analyzing metrics such as viewership, engagement, and audience retention. Use these insights to inform your future live streaming strategy and refine your content for maximum impact.

By incorporating live streaming into your social media strategy and leveraging these strategies, you can create real-time connections with your audience, foster engagement, and enhance your overall online presence. In the following chapters, we'll continue to explore strategies for optimizing your social media growth and harnessing the power of various content formats and platforms.

Chapter 7: The Art of Social Listening

7.1 Defining Social Listening

Social listening is the process of monitoring and analyzing conversations across social media platforms to gain insights into your audience's sentiments, preferences, and needs. By understanding and responding to these conversations, brands can improve their products and services, address customer concerns, and build stronger relationships with their followers. In this section, we'll define social listening and discuss its importance in developing a successful social media strategy.

Social listening goes beyond merely tracking likes, shares, and comments on your content. It involves:

1. Identifying mentions: Monitor social media platforms for mentions of your brand, products, or services, as well as industry-related keywords or competitors. This helps you gain insights into how your audience perceives your brand and identifies opportunities for engagement or improvement.

2. Analyzing sentiment: Analyze the tone and sentiment of the conversations surrounding your brand, enabling you to understand the overall perception of your brand and identify areas of concern or praise.

3. Discovering trends: Keep track of emerging trends, topics, or challenges within your industry or niche, allowing you to adapt your content strategy accordingly and remain relevant in the ever-changing social media landscape.

4. Gaining insights into your audience: Understand your audience's preferences, pain points, and interests by monitoring

their conversations and interactions on social media. This enables you to tailor your content and marketing strategies to better resonate with your target audience.

5. Identifying influencers and brand advocates: Through social listening, you can uncover influencers and brand advocates within your industry or niche, providing opportunities for collaboration or leveraging their reach to expand your audience.

6. Monitoring competitors: Keep an eye on your competitors' social media presence, allowing you to identify their strengths and weaknesses and adjust your strategy accordingly.

7. Responding and engaging: Actively respond to mentions and engage in conversations about your brand, demonstrating your commitment to customer satisfaction and fostering stronger relationships with your audience.

By mastering the art of social listening, you can gain valuable insights into your audience, industry, and competitors, enabling you to develop more effective content and marketing strategies. In the following sections, we'll discuss tools and techniques for implementing social listening and leveraging these insights to drive growth on your social media platforms.

7.2 Monitoring Conversations and Trends

Effective social listening requires continuous monitoring of conversations and trends across various social media platforms. This enables you to stay informed about your audience's preferences, industry developments, and emerging opportunities for engagement. In this section, we'll discuss strategies for monitoring conversations and trends in order to enhance your social listening efforts.

1. Use social media monitoring tools: Utilize tools such as Hootsuite, Mention, Brandwatch, or Sprout Social to track mentions, keywords, and hashtags related to your brand, industry, or competitors. These tools can help you gather data, analyze sentiment, and identify trends more efficiently than manual monitoring.

2. Set up alerts and notifications: Configure alerts and notifications for specific keywords, hashtags, or mentions to ensure you stay informed about relevant conversations and trends in real-time.

3. Monitor industry-specific forums and communities: In addition to monitoring social media platforms, keep an eye on industry-specific forums, communities, and discussion boards, such as Reddit, Quora, or niche Facebook groups. This can help you uncover valuable insights and identify emerging trends within your industry.

4. Track trending topics: Regularly check trending topics on platforms like Twitter, Instagram, and LinkedIn to stay up-to-date with current events, viral content, and popular conversations within your niche.

5. Conduct hashtag research: Research relevant hashtags within your industry or niche to identify popular and emerging trends. Monitor these hashtags to stay informed about the latest conversations and developments within your target audience.

6. Follow industry influencers and thought leaders: Stay updated on industry news, insights, and trends by following influential figures within your niche. Engage with their content and participate in discussions to establish your brand as an active member of your industry's community.

7. Analyze competitor activity: Keep an eye on your competitors' social media presence, content, and engagement strategies to identify their strengths, weaknesses, and opportunities for differentiation.

8. Schedule regular monitoring sessions: Dedicate time each day or week to review the data and insights gathered through your social listening efforts. This can help you stay informed about the latest conversations, trends, and developments within your industry and audience.

By implementing these monitoring strategies, you can enhance your social listening efforts and gain valuable insights that inform your content and marketing strategies. In the following sections, we'll discuss how to leverage these insights to drive growth on your social media platforms and optimize your overall strategy.

7.3 Identifying Influencers and Opportunities

An essential aspect of social listening is identifying key influencers and opportunities within your industry or niche. Collaborating with influencers or seizing emerging opportunities can help increase your brand's visibility, credibility, and reach. In this section, we'll discuss strategies for identifying influencers and opportunities through social listening.

1. Identify top-performing content: Analyze the most popular and engaging content within your niche to gain insights into the topics, formats, and creators that resonate with your target audience. This can help you identify influencers to collaborate with and uncover content opportunities for your brand.

2. Monitor mentions and engagement: Track the number and quality of mentions and engagements your brand receives on social media. Look for users who frequently mention or engage with your content, as they may be potential influencers or brand advocates.

3. Research industry-specific hashtags: Explore the most popular and relevant hashtags within your industry or niche to find influencers who are driving conversations and creating engaging content. Follow and engage with these influencers to build relationships and potential collaboration opportunities.

4. Use influencer identification tools: Leverage tools such as BuzzSumo, Klear, or NinjaOutreach to find influencers based on keywords, topics, or audience demographics. These tools can help you identify potential partners who align with your brand's values and goals.

5. Attend industry events and conferences: Participate in

industry events, conferences, and webinars to network with influencers, thought leaders, and potential partners. Engage in discussions and share your insights to establish your brand as a knowledgeable and influential presence within your niche.

6. Analyze competitor collaborations: Monitor your competitors' social media activity to identify influencers they are collaborating with or targeting. This can help you uncover potential partnership opportunities and stay informed about trends within your industry.

7. Evaluate influencer credibility and relevance: Before reaching out to influencers, evaluate their credibility, relevance, and audience demographics to ensure they align with your brand's goals and values. Consider factors such as engagement rate, content quality, and audience size when selecting potential partners.

8. Monitor emerging trends and conversations: Stay updated on the latest trends and conversations within your industry to identify opportunities for your brand to contribute, innovate, or lead the discussion. By being proactive and responsive to emerging trends, you can stay ahead of your competitors and establish your brand as a thought leader within your niche.

By identifying influencers and opportunities through social listening, you can develop strategic partnerships and capitalize on emerging trends to enhance your brand's visibility and credibility on social media. In the following sections, we'll discuss how to leverage these insights to optimize your content and marketing strategies, driving growth on your social media platforms.

7.4 Adapting to Real-Time Feedback

One of the major advantages of social listening is the ability to receive and respond to real-time feedback from your audience. By adapting your social media strategy based on this feedback, you can optimize your content, address concerns, and ultimately foster stronger relationships with your followers. In this section, we'll discuss strategies for adapting to real-time feedback through social listening.

1. Monitor and respond to comments: Actively monitor comments on your social media posts and respond to questions, concerns, or feedback in a timely manner. This demonstrates your commitment to customer satisfaction and encourages further engagement from your audience.

2. Address negative feedback proactively: Do not shy away from negative feedback or criticism. Instead, address it professionally and constructively, offering solutions or explanations where appropriate. This can help improve your brand's reputation and turn potential detractors into advocates.

3. Utilize direct messaging: Engage with your audience through direct messaging to address concerns or feedback on a more personal level. This can help build trust and rapport with your followers, demonstrating your genuine interest in their opinions and experiences.

4. Adjust your content strategy: Analyze the feedback received through social listening to identify patterns or trends in your audience's preferences. Use this information to adapt your content strategy, focusing on topics, formats, or platforms that resonate most with your target audience.

5. Learn from your competitors: Monitor your competitors' social media presence and analyze the feedback they receive from their audience. Use this information to identify areas where your brand can differentiate itself or capitalize on unaddressed customer needs.

6. Implement changes and track results: As you adapt your strategy based on real-time feedback, be sure to track the results of your changes. Analyze metrics such as engagement, reach, and sentiment to determine the effectiveness of your adjustments and identify areas for further improvement.

7. Communicate changes to your audience: Let your audience know that you value their feedback and are taking steps to address their concerns or suggestions. This can help build trust and loyalty with your followers, encouraging continued engagement and feedback in the future.

8. Continuously refine your strategy: Social listening is an ongoing process, and your strategy should continuously evolve based on the feedback and insights you receive. Regularly review and update your content and marketing strategies to ensure they remain relevant and effective in engaging your target audience.

By adapting to real-time feedback through social listening, you can optimize your social media strategy to better serve your audience and foster stronger relationships with your followers. In the following sections, we'll continue to explore strategies for driving growth on your social media platforms and harnessing the power of social listening to enhance your online presence.

7.5 Integrating Social Listening into Your Strategy

To fully capitalize on the benefits of social listening, it's crucial to integrate it into your overall social media strategy. This involves incorporating the insights and feedback gained from social listening into your content creation, engagement, and marketing efforts. In this section, we'll discuss strategies for integrating social listening into your strategy to drive growth and enhance your online presence.

1. Assign dedicated resources: Ensure that you have dedicated resources in place to manage and execute your social listening efforts. This may include assigning specific team members to monitor conversations, analyze data, and respond to feedback, or utilizing social media management tools to streamline these tasks.

2. Set clear objectives: Establish clear objectives for your social listening efforts, such as improving customer satisfaction, increasing engagement, identifying opportunities for collaboration, or uncovering industry trends. By setting specific goals, you can better align your social listening activities with your overall social media strategy.

3. Establish a feedback loop: Create a process for sharing insights and feedback gained from social listening with relevant team members, such as content creators, customer support representatives, or product managers. This enables your team to make informed decisions and adapt their strategies based on real-time feedback from your audience.

4. Regularly review and update your strategy: Incorporate regular reviews of your social listening data into your strategy development process. This allows you to continuously refine your content, engagement, and marketing strategies based on the

latest insights and feedback from your audience.

5. Create audience personas: Use the insights gained from social listening to develop detailed audience personas that reflect the preferences, needs, and behaviors of your target audience. This can help guide your content creation, targeting, and messaging strategies, ensuring they resonate with your audience and drive engagement.

6. Monitor and measure success: Establish key performance indicators (KPIs) to measure the success of your social listening efforts, such as sentiment analysis, engagement rate, or audience growth. Regularly track and analyze these metrics to determine the effectiveness of your social listening activities and inform future strategy decisions.

7. Be agile and responsive: Stay agile and responsive to the insights and feedback gained from social listening. Be prepared to adjust your strategy or tactics quickly when new trends, opportunities, or challenges arise, ensuring your brand remains relevant and engaging in the ever-changing social media landscape.

By integrating social listening into your overall social media strategy, you can leverage the insights and feedback gained from your audience to create more relevant, engaging, and effective content and marketing campaigns. This, in turn, can help drive growth on your social media platforms and enhance your brand's online presence.

Chapter 8: Succeeding with Paid Advertising

8.1 Exploring the World of Social Media Ads

Paid advertising is a powerful tool that can help you amplify your brand's reach, boost engagement, and drive conversions on social media platforms. To succeed with paid advertising, it's essential to understand the various ad formats, targeting options, and strategies that can maximize your return on investment (ROI). In this section, we'll provide an overview of the world of social media ads and discuss how to leverage them effectively.

1. Familiarize yourself with ad formats: Each social media platform offers a variety of ad formats, such as image ads, video ads, carousel ads, or sponsored posts. Familiarize yourself with the ad formats available on each platform and choose the one that best aligns with your campaign objectives and content strategy.

2. Define your campaign goals: Before launching a paid advertising campaign, establish clear goals, such as increasing brand awareness, driving website traffic, generating leads, or boosting sales. This will help guide your ad creation, targeting, and budgeting decisions.

3. Understand targeting options: Social media platforms offer a wealth of targeting options, allowing you to reach users based on demographics, interests, behaviors, and more. Understand the targeting options available on each platform and use them to create highly targeted campaigns that resonate with your ideal audience.

4. Set a budget and bid strategy: Determine a budget for your advertising campaign and decide on a bidding strategy, such as

cost-per-click (CPC), cost-per-impression (CPM), or cost-per-action (CPA). This will help ensure that you're spending your advertising dollars wisely and optimizing your ROI.

5. Develop compelling ad creatives: Create eye-catching and engaging ad creatives that capture your audience's attention and encourage them to take action. Use strong visuals, clear messaging, and a compelling call-to-action (CTA) to drive results.

6. Test and optimize your ads: Continuously test and optimize your ads to improve performance and maximize ROI. Experiment with different ad formats, targeting options, creatives, and bidding strategies to identify the most effective combinations for your campaign goals.

7. Monitor and analyze performance: Track the performance of your advertising campaigns using platform-specific analytics tools, such as Facebook Ads Manager or LinkedIn Campaign Manager. Analyze key metrics, such as impressions, clicks, conversions, and ROI, to measure the success of your campaigns and inform future strategy decisions.

By exploring the world of social media ads and implementing these strategies, you can create highly targeted, effective advertising campaigns that drive growth and achieve your marketing goals on social media platforms. In the following sections, we'll delve deeper into paid advertising strategies and discuss how to optimize your campaigns for success.

8.2 Crafting a Successful Ad Campaign

A well-crafted ad campaign is essential for achieving your marketing goals on social media platforms. To create a successful ad campaign, you'll need to combine effective targeting, compelling ad creatives, and smart budgeting with continuous optimization and analysis. In this section, we'll discuss strategies for crafting a successful ad campaign on social media.

1. Define your target audience: Clearly identify your target audience based on demographics, interests, behaviors, and other relevant factors. This will help you create personalized and relevant ad campaigns that resonate with your ideal customers and drive results.

2. Establish a clear message and call-to-action: Determine the primary message and call-to-action (CTA) for your ad campaign. Your message should be concise, engaging, and aligned with your campaign goals, while your CTA should clearly communicate the desired action you want your audience to take.

3. Select the right ad format: Choose the ad format that best suits your campaign objectives and content strategy. Consider factors such as platform-specific best practices, user preferences, and the type of content you're promoting when selecting an ad format.

4. Develop engaging ad creatives: Create visually appealing and engaging ad creatives that capture your audience's attention and convey your message effectively. Use high-quality images or videos, compelling headlines, and concise copy to encourage users to engage with your ads.

5. Optimize your landing pages: Ensure that your landing pages are optimized for conversions, with clear messaging, easy

navigation, and a strong call-to-action. A well-designed landing page can significantly improve the performance of your ad campaign by increasing conversion rates and reducing bounce rates.

6. Set a strategic budget and bid: Allocate a budget for your ad campaign based on your marketing goals and target audience size. Choose a bidding strategy, such as cost-per-click (CPC), cost-per-impression (CPM), or cost-per-action (CPA), that aligns with your campaign objectives and helps you maximize ROI.

7. Test and iterate: Launch your ad campaign and monitor its performance closely. Experiment with different ad creatives, targeting options, and bidding strategies to identify the most effective combinations for achieving your campaign goals. Continuously optimize your campaign based on data-driven insights to improve performance and ROI.

8. Measure and analyze results: Use platform-specific analytics tools to track and analyze the performance of your ad campaign. Focus on key metrics, such as impressions, clicks, conversions, and ROI, to measure success and inform future campaign decisions.

By following these strategies, you can craft a successful ad campaign on social media platforms that drives growth and achieves your marketing goals. In the next sections, we'll continue to explore paid advertising strategies and discuss how to further optimize your campaigns for success.

8.3 Targeting Your Ideal Audience

One of the most critical aspects of a successful social media ad campaign is targeting the right audience. Effective targeting ensures that your ads are shown to users who are most likely to engage with your content and take the desired action. In this section, we'll discuss strategies for targeting your ideal audience on social media platforms.

1. Identify your target audience: Start by clearly defining your target audience based on demographics, interests, behaviors, and other relevant factors. This information will help you create personalized and relevant ad campaigns that resonate with your ideal customers.

2. Utilize platform-specific targeting options: Each social media platform offers a range of targeting options that can help you refine your audience. These may include demographic targeting, interest-based targeting, behavior targeting, and custom audiences. Familiarize yourself with the targeting options available on each platform and use them to create highly targeted ad campaigns.

3. Create custom audiences: Many social media platforms allow you to create custom audiences based on your existing customer data, such as email addresses, phone numbers, or website visitors. By creating custom audiences, you can target users who have already expressed interest in your brand, increasing the likelihood of engagement and conversions.

4. Employ lookalike audiences: Lookalike audiences are groups of users who share similar characteristics with your existing customers. Many social media platforms offer the option to create lookalike audiences based on your custom audiences, allowing you to reach new users who are likely to be interested in your

brand.

5. Segment your audience: Break down your target audience into smaller, more specific segments based on factors such as age, gender, location, interests, or behaviors. By segmenting your audience, you can create more personalized and relevant ad campaigns that cater to the unique needs and preferences of each group.

6. Test and refine targeting: Continuously test and refine your targeting options to identify the most effective combinations for reaching your ideal audience. Experiment with different audience segments, targeting options, and platforms to determine which approaches yield the best results.

7. Monitor and analyze performance: Use platform-specific analytics tools to track and analyze the performance of your ad campaigns across different audience segments and targeting options. Focus on key metrics, such as impressions, clicks, conversions, and ROI, to measure success and inform future targeting decisions.

By implementing these targeting strategies, you can ensure that your social media ad campaigns reach your ideal audience, maximizing engagement, conversions, and ROI. In the following sections, we'll continue to explore paid advertising strategies and discuss how to optimize your campaigns for success.

8.4 Optimizing Ad Performance

Optimizing ad performance is crucial for maximizing the return on investment (ROI) of your social media advertising campaigns. By continuously testing, analyzing, and refining your ads, you can improve their effectiveness and achieve your marketing goals. In this section, we'll discuss strategies for optimizing ad performance on social media platforms.

1. A/B test your ad creatives: Experiment with different ad creatives, such as images, videos, headlines, and ad copy, to determine which elements resonate most with your target audience. Run A/B tests to compare different variations of your ads and identify the most effective combinations.

2. Test different ad formats: Social media platforms offer a variety of ad formats, such as image ads, video ads, carousel ads, or sponsored posts. Test different ad formats to determine which ones perform best for your campaign objectives and content strategy.

3. Adjust your targeting options: Experiment with different targeting options, such as demographics, interests, behaviors, and custom audiences, to identify the most effective combinations for reaching your ideal audience. Continuously refine your targeting based on data-driven insights to improve ad performance.

4. Monitor ad frequency and ad fatigue: Keep an eye on ad frequency, which refers to the average number of times a user sees your ad within a specific time frame. High ad frequency can lead to ad fatigue, resulting in reduced engagement and conversions. Adjust your targeting, ad placements, and budget to prevent ad fatigue and maintain optimal ad performance.

5. Optimize your bidding strategy: Experiment with different bidding strategies, such as cost-per-click (CPC), cost-per-impression (CPM), or cost-per-action (CPA), to find the most cost-effective approach for achieving your campaign goals. Adjust your bids based on ad performance and competition to maximize ROI.

6. Review and optimize ad placements: Social media platforms offer various ad placements, such as news feed, stories, or in-app ads. Analyze the performance of your ads across different placements and make necessary adjustments to improve visibility and engagement.

7. Leverage social media management tools: Use social media management tools, such as Hootsuite, Buffer, or Sprout Social, to streamline your ad campaign management, analysis, and optimization efforts. These tools can help you automate tasks, track performance, and identify opportunities for improvement.

8. Analyze and learn from campaign data: Regularly review your ad campaign data using platform-specific analytics tools. Focus on key performance indicators (KPIs), such as impressions, clicks, conversions, and ROI, to measure success and identify areas for improvement.

By implementing these optimization strategies, you can continually improve the performance of your social media ad campaigns, driving engagement, conversions, and ROI. In the next sections, we'll continue to explore paid advertising strategies and discuss additional tactics for maximizing your success on social media platforms.

8.5 Measuring Return on Investment

Measuring the return on investment (ROI) of your social media advertising campaigns is essential for evaluating their success and making data-driven decisions. By tracking ROI, you can assess the effectiveness of your campaigns, identify areas for improvement, and allocate resources more efficiently. In this section, we'll discuss strategies for measuring ROI on social media ad campaigns.

1. Set clear campaign objectives: Establish specific, measurable, attainable, relevant, and time-bound (SMART) objectives for your ad campaigns. These objectives will serve as the foundation for assessing the ROI of your campaigns and can include goals such as increasing website traffic, generating leads, or driving sales.

2. Determine key performance indicators (KPIs): Identify the KPIs that align with your campaign objectives and reflect the success of your advertising efforts. Common KPIs for social media advertising include impressions, clicks, click-through rate (CTR), conversions, and cost per action (CPA).

3. Calculate your ad spend: Track the total amount you're spending on your social media ad campaigns, including ad costs, creative development, and management fees. This information will help you determine the cost-effectiveness of your campaigns and calculate your ROI.

4. Monitor revenue and conversions: Measure the revenue generated from your ad campaigns by tracking conversions, such as leads, sign-ups, or sales. Use platform-specific analytics tools, along with website and e-commerce tracking tools, to accurately attribute revenue to your advertising efforts.

5. Calculate ROI: Determine the ROI of your social media advertising campaigns by comparing the revenue generated to your total ad spend. Use the formula: ROI = (Revenue - Ad Spend) / Ad Spend * 100. A positive ROI indicates that your ad campaigns are generating a profit, while a negative ROI signals a need for optimization and improvement.

6. Benchmark against industry standards: Compare your ad campaign performance and ROI to industry benchmarks to gauge your success relative to competitors. This information can help you identify areas where you're excelling or falling behind and inform your future marketing decisions.

7. Continuously optimize your campaigns: Use the insights gathered from measuring ROI to optimize your ad campaigns for improved performance. Test different ad creatives, targeting options, and bidding strategies to identify the most effective combinations for achieving your marketing goals and maximizing ROI.

8. Evaluate long-term value: In addition to immediate ROI, consider the long-term value of your social media advertising efforts. This can include factors such as customer lifetime value (CLV), brand awareness, and customer loyalty, which contribute to the overall success of your marketing strategy.

By measuring ROI and implementing data-driven optimization strategies, you can maximize the effectiveness of your social media advertising campaigns and achieve your marketing goals. In the following chapters, we'll continue to explore strategies for success on social media platforms and discuss additional tactics for driving growth and engagement.

Chapter 9: Navigating the Legal Landscape

9.1 Understanding Copyright and Intellectual Property

As you grow your presence on social media and create content to engage your audience, it's essential to understand the legal aspects of copyright and intellectual property. This knowledge will help you protect your own creative works and ensure that you're respecting the rights of others. In this section, we'll discuss the basics of copyright and intellectual property in the context of social media.

1. Copyright basics: Copyright is a legal protection that grants the creator of an original work exclusive rights to its use and distribution. This applies to various forms of creative content, such as text, images, videos, and music. When you create original content for your social media channels, you automatically hold the copyright to that content.

2. Intellectual property: Intellectual property (IP) refers to creations of the mind, such as inventions, artistic works, designs, and symbols. IP is protected by various legal mechanisms, including copyrights, patents, and trademarks. Understanding the different types of IP protection is crucial for safeguarding your creative assets and avoiding potential legal issues.

3. Fair use and exceptions: In some cases, you may be permitted to use copyrighted material without obtaining permission from the copyright holder. This concept is known as fair use and typically applies to situations where the use is transformative, such as commentary, criticism, parody, or news reporting. However, fair use is a complex legal concept, and its application can vary depending on the circumstances. Consult with a legal expert if you're unsure whether your use of copyrighted material falls

under fair use.

4. User-generated content: User-generated content (UGC) refers to any content created by users, such as comments, reviews, or social media posts. While sharing UGC can be an effective way to engage your audience and build your brand, it's essential to ensure that you have the necessary permissions to use and share this content, especially if it contains copyrighted material.

5. Licensing and permissions: If you want to use copyrighted material in your social media content, you may need to obtain a license or permission from the copyright holder. This can include purchasing stock images or music, obtaining a Creative Commons license, or directly contacting the copyright owner for permission.

6. Protecting your own content: To protect your own copyrighted content, consider registering your works with the appropriate authorities, such as the U.S. Copyright Office. Additionally, include copyright notices on your content and monitor the use of your creative works on social media to identify and address potential infringement.

7. Trademarks and branding: Trademarks are a type of intellectual property that protects words, phrases, symbols, or designs that identify and distinguish the source of goods or services. Registering your brand's name, logo, or slogan as a trademark can help protect your brand identity and prevent others from using similar marks that may cause confusion.

By understanding copyright and intellectual property in the context of social media, you can create and share content with confidence, protect your creative assets, and respect the rights of others. In the next sections, we'll continue to explore the legal landscape and discuss additional legal considerations for social media marketing, such as privacy and disclosure requirements.

9.2 Complying with Advertising Regulations

In addition to understanding copyright and intellectual property, it's crucial to comply with advertising regulations and guidelines when promoting your brand on social media. These regulations are designed to ensure transparency, protect consumers, and maintain a fair marketplace. In this section, we'll discuss key aspects of advertising regulations in the context of social media marketing.

1. Disclosure of sponsored content: When partnering with influencers or creating sponsored content, it's essential to disclose the commercial relationship between your brand and the content creator. This can be achieved by using clear and conspicuous disclosures, such as hashtags like #ad, #sponsored, or #partner. These disclosures help maintain transparency and ensure that consumers can easily identify paid content.

2. Endorsements and testimonials: If your social media marketing strategy involves endorsements or testimonials, ensure that they are truthful and not misleading. Endorsers must have a genuine experience with the product or service and should not make claims that cannot be substantiated. Additionally, any material connections between the endorser and your brand must be disclosed.

3. Compliance with platform-specific guidelines: Each social media platform has its own set of advertising guidelines and policies. Familiarize yourself with these guidelines and ensure that your marketing efforts comply with the specific requirements of each platform. This may include restrictions on certain types of content, targeting options, or ad formats.

4. Data privacy and protection: As a marketer, it's essential to adhere to data privacy regulations, such as the General Data

Protection Regulation (GDPR) in the European Union or the California Consumer Privacy Act (CCPA) in the United States. These regulations require businesses to protect user data, provide transparency regarding data collection and usage, and obtain consent for data processing.

5. Compliance with industry-specific regulations: Depending on your industry, there may be additional advertising regulations that apply to your social media marketing efforts. For example, healthcare, financial services, and alcohol industries are often subject to strict advertising guidelines. Ensure that you're aware of and comply with any industry-specific regulations that pertain to your business.

6. Avoiding deceptive practices: Be mindful of advertising practices that could be considered deceptive or misleading, such as using clickbait headlines, making false claims, or manipulating user reviews. Engaging in deceptive practices can harm your brand's reputation and may result in legal consequences.

By complying with advertising regulations and guidelines, you can maintain a transparent and ethical social media marketing strategy that protects consumers and fosters trust in your brand. In the next sections, we'll continue to explore the legal landscape and discuss additional legal considerations for social media marketing, such as user privacy and protecting your brand's reputation.

9.3 Protecting Your Brand and Reputation

Safeguarding your brand's reputation is an essential aspect of social media marketing. A positive brand image can help you build trust with your audience, attract new customers, and foster long-term loyalty. In this section, we'll discuss strategies for protecting your brand and maintaining a strong reputation on social media.

1. Monitor your brand's online presence: Keep an eye on mentions of your brand across social media platforms, review sites, and other online channels. This will help you stay informed about public perception, identify potential issues, and address any negative feedback or concerns in a timely manner.

2. Address negative feedback constructively: When faced with negative comments or reviews, respond professionally and empathetically. Acknowledge the issue, provide an explanation or solution, and thank the person for their feedback. By demonstrating that you value your customers' opinions and are committed to improving, you can help mitigate the impact of negative feedback on your brand's reputation.

3. Develop a crisis management plan: Be prepared for potential crises, such as negative press coverage, product recalls, or social media controversies. Develop a crisis management plan that outlines clear steps for addressing the issue, communicating with stakeholders, and mitigating damage to your brand's reputation.

4. Maintain consistent brand messaging: Ensure that your brand messaging is consistent across all social media platforms, as well as other marketing channels. This consistency will help establish a strong brand identity and prevent confusion among your audience.

5. Be transparent and authentic: Cultivate an authentic and transparent brand image by being open about your business practices, values, and goals. This can help foster trust and loyalty among your audience and strengthen your brand's reputation.

6. Establish clear social media guidelines: Develop a set of guidelines for your employees and partners to follow when representing your brand on social media. These guidelines should outline expectations for professional conduct, content creation, and engagement with your audience.

7. Take legal precautions: Protect your brand's intellectual property, such as trademarks and copyrights, by registering them with the appropriate authorities. Additionally, stay informed about advertising regulations and ensure that your social media marketing efforts comply with these guidelines.

By taking proactive steps to protect your brand and maintain a strong reputation on social media, you can foster trust with your audience and support the long-term success of your marketing efforts. In the following chapter, we'll explore additional strategies for growth on social media and discuss tactics for staying ahead of the competition.

9.4 Addressing Privacy and Security Concerns

Privacy and security concerns are becoming increasingly important in the digital age, and addressing these issues is an essential aspect of responsible social media marketing. In this section, we'll discuss strategies for safeguarding user privacy, securing your online presence, and building trust with your audience.

1. Implement robust privacy policies: Develop clear and transparent privacy policies that outline how your organization collects, uses, stores, and shares user data. Ensure that your privacy policies comply with relevant data protection regulations, such as the General Data Protection Regulation (GDPR) or the California Consumer Privacy Act (CCPA).

2. Obtain user consent: When collecting personal information from users, obtain their explicit consent and provide them with the option to opt-out of data collection and processing. This can help foster trust and demonstrate your commitment to protecting user privacy.

3. Protect user data: Implement strong security measures to safeguard the personal information of your users, such as encryption, secure storage, and access controls. Regularly review and update your security practices to stay current with evolving threats and best practices.

4. Educate your team: Provide training and resources for your employees and partners to ensure they understand the importance of privacy and security and follow best practices when handling user data and engaging on social media.

5. Be transparent about data breaches: In the event of a data

breach or security incident, notify affected users promptly and provide information about the steps you're taking to address the issue. Being transparent about security incidents can help mitigate damage to your brand's reputation and demonstrate your commitment to user privacy.

6. Secure your social media accounts: Use strong, unique passwords for your social media accounts and enable two-factor authentication to protect against unauthorized access. Regularly review and update your account settings to ensure they align with best practices for security and privacy.

7. Monitor for potential threats: Keep an eye on your social media channels for signs of potential security threats, such as phishing attempts, spam, or malicious content. Implement tools and processes to identify and address these threats promptly, and educate your audience about potential risks and how to protect themselves.

By addressing privacy and security concerns proactively, you can demonstrate your commitment to responsible social media marketing and build trust with your audience. In the final chapter, we'll explore strategies for staying ahead of the competition and adapting to the ever-evolving landscape of social media.

9.5 Staying Informed on Legal Changes

As social media continues to evolve, so do the legal and regulatory landscapes surrounding it. To ensure that your marketing efforts remain compliant and protect your brand's reputation, it's essential to stay informed about changes to relevant laws, regulations, and industry best practices. In this section, we'll discuss strategies for staying up-to-date with legal changes that affect your social media marketing efforts.

1. Subscribe to industry newsletters and updates: Sign up for newsletters and updates from legal, marketing, and industry-specific sources. These resources can help keep you informed about changes to laws, regulations, and best practices that may impact your social media marketing strategy.

2. Follow relevant organizations and authorities: Stay connected with regulatory bodies, industry associations, and legal organizations on social media and other platforms. These organizations often share updates, news, and insights about changes to the legal landscape that may affect your business.

3. Attend industry conferences and events: Participate in conferences, webinars, and other industry events to stay informed about emerging trends, best practices, and legal changes. Networking with other professionals in your industry can also provide valuable insights and perspectives on navigating the evolving legal landscape.

4. Consult with legal experts: Establish a relationship with a legal professional or firm that specializes in your industry or the area of law relevant to your social media marketing efforts. Regularly consult with these experts to ensure that your marketing strategy remains compliant and up-to-date with the latest legal requirements.

5. Monitor changes to platform-specific guidelines: Keep an eye on updates and changes to the advertising and content guidelines for each social media platform you use. These platforms often update their policies to reflect changes in the legal landscape or to address emerging issues, so it's essential to stay informed about these updates and adjust your strategy accordingly.

6. Provide ongoing training for your team: Ensure that your team members receive regular training and updates about changes to laws, regulations, and best practices that affect your social media marketing efforts. Providing ongoing education can help your team stay informed and adapt more easily to changes in the legal landscape.

By staying informed about legal changes and adapting your social media marketing strategy accordingly, you can protect your brand's reputation, maintain compliance, and continue to grow your audience in an ever-evolving digital landscape.

Chapter 10: Future-Proofing Your Social Media Strategy

10.1 Embracing Platform Changes and Updates

As social media platforms continue to evolve, it's essential to adapt your marketing strategy to leverage new features, changes, and updates. Staying ahead of the curve will enable you to maintain a competitive edge and ensure that your efforts remain effective in a constantly changing digital landscape. In this section, we'll discuss strategies for embracing platform changes and updates to future-proof your social media strategy.

1. Monitor platform updates: Keep an eye on announcements from social media platforms regarding new features, updates, and changes to their algorithms. Being aware of these changes will allow you to adjust your strategy proactively and make the most of new opportunities.

2. Experiment with new features: When a platform introduces a new feature, be one of the first to test it out and assess its potential impact on your marketing efforts. Early adoption of new features can provide a competitive advantage and help you stay ahead of the curve.

3. Adapt your content strategy: As platforms evolve, the types of content that perform well may change. Stay informed about emerging content trends and adapt your content strategy accordingly. This may involve experimenting with new formats, such as short-form video, or focusing on new engagement metrics.

4. Stay informed about algorithm changes: Social media platforms regularly update their algorithms, which can have a significant

impact on your content's reach and visibility. Stay informed about these changes and adjust your posting strategy, content mix, and engagement tactics to ensure your content continues to reach your target audience.

5. Be platform-agnostic: While it's essential to master the intricacies of each platform, don't become overly reliant on a single platform for your marketing success. Diversify your social media presence across multiple platforms to minimize the impact of platform-specific changes and updates on your overall strategy.

6. Engage with platform communities: Participate in platform-specific forums, groups, or communities to stay informed about changes, updates, and best practices. Engaging with these communities can provide valuable insights and help you stay ahead of the curve when it comes to platform changes.

7. Stay agile and adaptable: Social media is an ever-evolving landscape, and your marketing strategy should be just as flexible. Be prepared to pivot and adapt your strategy as needed to respond to changes and updates on various platforms. This may involve reallocating resources, experimenting with new tactics, or shifting your focus to emerging platforms.

By embracing platform changes and updates, you can ensure that your social media marketing strategy remains effective and relevant in a constantly evolving digital landscape. In the next sections, we'll explore additional strategies for future-proofing your social media marketing efforts.

10.2 Adapting to Evolving User Behavior

As social media platforms change, so do the behaviors and preferences of their users. Adapting your social media strategy to keep pace with these evolving trends is essential for maintaining a strong online presence and continuing to engage your target audience. In this section, we'll discuss strategies for adapting to evolving user behavior and ensuring that your marketing efforts remain relevant and effective.

1. Monitor audience behaviour: Regularly analyze your audience insights to identify any shifts in user behavior, such as changes in content preferences, engagement patterns, or demographics. Use this information to inform your content strategy and ensure that your efforts continue to resonate with your target audience.

2. Conduct regular surveys and polls: Engage with your audience directly to gather feedback on their preferences, needs, and interests. Use surveys, polls, or other feedback mechanisms to collect this information and adjust your social media strategy accordingly.

3. Stay informed about industry trends: Keep an eye on emerging trends within your industry and niche, as these can influence user behavior and expectations. By staying informed about these trends, you can adapt your social media strategy to better align with your audience's evolving interests and needs.

4. Experiment with content formats: As user behavior evolves, the types of content that resonate with your audience may change. Be prepared to experiment with different content formats, such as video, images, or interactive content, to determine what resonates best with your target audience.

5. Personalize your messaging: As users become more discerning in their consumption of social media content, personalized messaging becomes increasingly important. Use audience insights and data to tailor your content and messaging to the unique needs and preferences of your target audience.

6. Optimize for mobile: With the increasing popularity of mobile devices, it's essential to ensure that your social media content is optimized for mobile consumption. This may involve adjusting your content formats, image sizes, or posting times to better suit the mobile experience.

7. Be responsive and adaptable: Stay responsive to changes in user behavior by continually testing and refining your social media strategy. This may involve adjusting your posting schedule, content mix, or engagement tactics based on your audience's evolving preferences and needs.

By adapting to evolving user behavior, you can ensure that your social media marketing efforts remain relevant and effective in an ever-changing digital landscape. In the following sections, we'll explore additional strategies for future-proofing your social media strategy.

10.3 Experimenting with Emerging Technologies

As technology continues to advance, new tools and platforms are constantly emerging, offering novel opportunities for brands to engage with their audiences on social media. Staying on the cutting edge of these emerging technologies can provide a competitive advantage and help you adapt your social media strategy to an ever-evolving digital landscape. In this section, we'll discuss strategies for experimenting with emerging technologies and incorporating them into your social media marketing efforts.

1. Stay informed about emerging technologies: Keep an eye on industry news and trends to stay informed about new technologies that have the potential to impact social media marketing. Attend conferences, follow thought leaders, and subscribe to industry newsletters to stay up-to-date on the latest technological advancements.

2. Assess the relevance of new technologies: Before investing time and resources into a new technology, assess its relevance to your brand and audience. Consider whether the technology offers a unique opportunity to engage with your target audience, aligns with your brand values, and has the potential to provide a meaningful return on investment.

3. Experiment with new tools and platforms: Be open to trying out new tools and platforms that can enhance your social media marketing efforts. This might include augmented reality (AR) or virtual reality (VR) experiences, chatbots, artificial intelligence (AI)-powered content creation tools, or other emerging technologies.

4. Pilot new technologies with a small audience: Before fully committing to a new technology, pilot it with a small, targeted audience to gauge its effectiveness and gather feedback. Use this

feedback to refine your approach and determine whether the technology is worth investing in further.

5. Collaborate with experts and partners: Seek out partnerships with experts, influencers, or other brands that have experience with emerging technologies. Collaborating with others can help you learn from their expertise, gain new insights, and explore innovative ways to leverage new technologies in your social media marketing efforts.

6. Measure the impact of new technologies: As you experiment with emerging technologies, be sure to measure their impact on your social media marketing goals. Use analytics and data to evaluate the success of your efforts, and use this information to inform your future investments in new technologies.

7. Be prepared to adapt and pivot: As with any aspect of social media marketing, be prepared to adapt and pivot your strategy as you experiment with emerging technologies. Some technologies may not deliver the results you anticipated, while others may exceed your expectations. Stay agile and be willing to adjust your approach based on the results you observe.

By experimenting with emerging technologies and incorporating them into your social media marketing efforts, you can stay ahead of the curve and ensure your strategy remains relevant and effective in a constantly evolving digital landscape. In the next sections, we'll explore additional strategies for future-proofing your social media strategy.

10.4 Continuously Learning and Updating Your Skills

The digital landscape is constantly evolving, and staying up-to-date with the latest trends, tools, and best practices is essential for maintaining a successful social media marketing strategy. In this section, we'll discuss strategies for continuously learning and updating your skills to ensure that your social media efforts remain effective and relevant in an ever-changing environment.

1. Stay informed about industry news and trends: Regularly follow industry news, blogs, and thought leaders to stay informed about the latest trends, platform updates, and best practices in social media marketing. This will help you stay ahead of the curve and adapt your strategy as needed.

2. Attend conferences and webinars: Participate in industry conferences, webinars, and workshops to deepen your understanding of social media marketing and stay current with the latest tools, strategies, and best practices. These events can also be valuable networking opportunities, allowing you to connect with other professionals and learn from their experiences.

3. Enroll in online courses and certifications: Invest in your professional development by enrolling in online courses and earning certifications in social media marketing. This can help you deepen your understanding of the field, stay current with the latest trends, and demonstrate your expertise to potential clients or employers.

4. Join industry groups and communities: Participate in social media marketing groups, forums, or communities to engage with other professionals, share knowledge, and learn from the experiences of others. These communities can be a valuable source of support, inspiration, and information, helping you

stay informed and up-to-date on the latest developments in the industry.

5. Experiment with new tools and techniques: Be open to trying new tools, platforms, and techniques to expand your skillset and stay current with the latest trends in social media marketing. This might involve experimenting with new content formats, leveraging emerging technologies, or adopting new engagement tactics.

6. Seek feedback and mentorship: Actively seek feedback from peers, colleagues, or mentors to identify areas for growth and improvement in your social media marketing efforts. This can help you refine your approach, learn from the experiences of others, and continuously improve your skills.

7. Allocate time for learning and skill development: Set aside regular time in your schedule for learning and skill development, whether it's attending webinars, reading industry news, or participating in online courses. By dedicating time to continuous learning, you can ensure that your social media marketing skills remain current and effective.

By continuously learning and updating your skills, you can ensure that your social media marketing efforts remain relevant and effective in an ever-changing digital landscape. In the next sections, we'll explore additional strategies for future-proofing your social media strategy.

10.5 Cultivating a Growth Mindset and Embracing Innovation

A growth mindset, characterized by a willingness to learn, adapt, and innovate, is essential for navigating the ever-changing landscape of social media marketing. In this section, we'll discuss strategies for cultivating a growth mindset and embracing innovation, enabling you to continuously evolve your social media strategy and stay ahead of the curve.

1. Be open to change: Recognize that change is inevitable in the world of social media and be open to adapting your strategy as platforms, technologies, and user behaviors evolve. Embrace change as an opportunity to learn, grow, and improve your social media marketing efforts.

2. Seek out new ideas and perspectives: Actively seek out new ideas, perspectives, and inspiration from a variety of sources, including industry thought leaders, peers, and even competitors. This can help you stay informed about the latest trends, spark creativity, and inspire innovation in your social media strategy.

3. Challenge assumptions and test hypotheses: Continuously question your assumptions about what works in social media marketing and be willing to test new hypotheses. This can involve experimenting with new content formats, engagement tactics, or targeting strategies to see what drives the best results for your brand.

4. Learn from failures and setbacks: Embrace failures and setbacks as valuable learning opportunities, rather than seeing them as negative experiences. By analyzing what went wrong and identifying areas for improvement, you can iterate on your strategy and continuously improve your social media marketing efforts.

5. Collaborate and share knowledge: Foster a culture of collaboration and knowledge-sharing within your team or organization. Encourage team members to share their ideas, experiences, and insights, and be open to learning from the expertise of others.

6. Embrace risk-taking and experimentation: Recognize that innovation often involves a certain level of risk-taking and be willing to experiment with new ideas, even if they might not succeed. By taking calculated risks and embracing a culture of experimentation, you can uncover new opportunities for growth and success in your social media marketing efforts.

7. Celebrate progress and growth: Acknowledge and celebrate the progress and growth you achieve in your social media marketing efforts, whether it's reaching a new milestone, implementing a successful campaign, or learning from a failed experiment. Recognizing these accomplishments can help reinforce a growth mindset and foster a culture of continuous improvement.

By cultivating a growth mindset and embracing innovation, you can ensure that your social media strategy remains relevant, effective, and agile in the face of constant change. By combining these strategies with the other future-proofing tactics discussed throughout this chapter, you can position your brand for continued success on social media, no matter what challenges the digital landscape presents.

www.ingramcontent.com/pod-product-compliance
Lightning Source LLC
Chambersburg PA
CBHW070653220526
45466CB00001B/421